TOWARDS INDEPENDENCE IN AFRICA

Patrick Walker caught the African 'bug' in early boyhood in Kenya and after Oxford and the 'Devonshire' course for the Overseas Civil Service, he served in Uganda from 1956 to 1962. On leaving the Colonial Service he joined MI5 where he was Director-General from 1988 to 1992.

TOWARDS INDEPENDENCE IN AFRICA

A District Officer in Uganda at the End of Empire

PATRICK WALKER

The Radcliffe Press
LONDON • NEW YORK

Published in 2009 by I.B.Tauris & Co. Ltd
6 Salem Road, London W2 4BU
175 Fifth Avenue, New York NY 10010
Website: http://www.ibtauris.com

Distributed in the United States and Canada Exclusively by Palgrave
Macmillan, 175 Fifth Avenue, New York NY 10010

ISBN 978 1 84885 019 4

A full CIP record for this book is available from the British Library
A full CIP record for this book is available from the Library of Congress
Library of Congress catalog card: available

Typeset in Garamond by Dexter Haven Associates Ltd, London
Printed and bound in Great Britain by CPI Antony Rowe, Chippenham

For Susan

Contents

List of Illustrations   ix
Preface   xi

1.   Family Background   1

2.   Malaya   11

3.   Kenya Childhood   23

4.   Preparatory School (Kenton College)   35

5.   Transition (King's School, Canterbury)   50

6.   Starting a Career: Devonshire Course   67

7.   Teso District   79

8.   Long Leave   151

9.   Ankole District   154

10. Refugees   171

11. Politics and Religion   177

12. Social Life and End of Tour   188

13. Conclusions   198

Annex 1: Guidance to ADCs on Changes to the Constitution   205
Annex 2: Handover Notes for Arms and Ammunition   211
Annex 3: Letter of Resignation   213
Annex 4: 1985 Letter from Uganda Army Wives   215
Index   217

List of Illustrations

Plumer Cosby Walker, my grandfather   3

Florence Ellen Walker, my father's sister   4

My mother as district nurse   8

My father outside his bungalow   13

The sports car   16

Railway offices, Kuala Lumpur   16

My parents' wedding, 1927   17

The family and cars in Sayers Road – my playroom
over the porch   18

My third birthday, dressed as Cupid   21

Rita Thompson   24

No. 1 Ngong Road   26

The 1936 Dodge outside the Nairobi Club   31

My father in his office in Nairobi   32

The private carriage at Athi River 1948   33

Westwood Park   37

Meister Omers   54

My parents, 1945   55

Scoring for Oxford, 1952   63

My parents with Susan, Adrian and Rob Beith   75

Soroti House, 1957   80

Soroti House, 1996   81

Soroti from the Rock   83

Ludya with Adrian   87

Going to the Lira riot 95

Soroti Club, 1957 102

The dancing beginning 104

The feast begins, Bukedea County Show 105

Bushman paintings on Ngora Rock 106

Salatieri supervising Juma at Atetur rest camp 106

Ngino rest camp on our first safari 108

In safari dress, Atetur rest camp, November 1956 110

Usuku homestead (photo: Edward Cunningham) 123

Checking voting application forms with the chiefs 128

Swearing in polling staff 128

Limuru Hunt 129

Adrian, Christmas 1958 137

Perseus and Medusa. The Roman is Paddy Foley – his helmet 138
an inverted cake stand

The winner 138

Loading the porters on Napak 146

Porters resting on Napak 147

House no. 1, Mbarara 155

Christmas 1960 160

Mbarara club, 1996 161

Katunguru Regatta (photo: Peter Herbert) 162

Ankole cattle (photo: Peter Herbert) 166

Kisoro resettlement meeting (with Hugh Fraser) 167

Oruchinga refugee camp: administration centre 174

Oruchinga camp: a new section 175

Bishop Ogez 180

Typing the election registers 184

Crossing the line 195

The Holdens and us with the captain 196

Preface

During my service in MI5, especially during my time as its Director General, I made a number of trips overseas, but none to Africa. After retirement I became involved in Leonard Cheshire, the organisation working with disabled people in many countries. It was as its International Chairman from 1995 to 2000 that my wife, Susan, and I returned to Uganda in 1996 and 2000. Under President Museveni the country was recovering from the Amin and Obote years. Susan and I were able to go to the two districts in which we had served and saw our old homes. The visits encouraged me to start writing about my life overseas.

I hope these recollections will show how, in a roundabout way, a colonial childhood drew me back to Africa and, in the chapters on Uganda, what it was like to be a young married District Officer in the years immediately before independence.

To evoke life in Malaya and Kenya I have had to rely on my memory, the rare descriptions from my parents of their lives and the few family records that survived. I hope that in this way I will be able to give some flavour of my parents' characters and of our life in both countries. I am also grateful to Charles Gardner for help over my prep school in Kenya, Kenton College.

For our time in Uganda I have relied heavily on letters which Susan (née Hastings) wrote to her mother and on her memory, which for many incidents is sharp and detailed. I am also grateful for the help given by Edward Cunningham, Peter Herbert and Keith Batten. Other sources are the papers I retained, including mileage logbooks.

The account of our life in Uganda is not a political history, though politics, especially their impact at ground level, are an important element. I hope that what the account will give is an impression of a way of life that has disappeared as seen through the eyes of a young Administrative Officer and his family, and of the kind of life led by officials and others on upcountry stations. Some may find the stories slightly frivolous but life was not all seriousness, thank goodness.

My parents were essentially uncommunicative. My father was not concerned about family history; he dismissed it as something that interested his brother, Cyril. Discussion of his and his family's past was not made easier by the fact that in 1945, at thirteen, I left Kenya to go to school in the UK (Kings School, Canterbury) and, unfortunately, when we met again in 1946 my relationship with him was not good enough to encourage me to want to talk to him. It would have required more willpower than I possessed as a difficult teenager and I was too short-sighted to make the attempt. Perhaps the situation was not made easier by the lack of a close relationship between my parents. They were fond of each other in their way. My mother was a cool, detached woman who viewed the world from her essentially self-centred though amused position. On the other hand, my father was driven by a social conscience which involved him in many activities in which my mother took no interest. Their communication seemed to me to be at a very superficial level. I say this not to excuse my self-centred absorption in my own life and activities, but to show that there was little volunteering of information which could have sparked my interest in their earlier lives or in their families.

I was brought up to keep myself out of my writing. Readers will understand this better when they have read the description of my parents. I have tried to describe my reaction to events but it is not easy to do so without it appearing contrived. For me, problems and difficulties had to be resolved by working through them. An overtly emotional response is not my style.

In reading these recollections it is important to remember that they relate to a way of life that has disappeared and show attitudes which, in this politically correct age, could be misunderstood. For instance, the use of the term 'houseboy' may offend, but it was the term in use and, as will be clear from the sections on servants, did not imply any disparagement of people for whom we had great affection. In the same way, the 'European' clubs would now be regarded as racist, but they fulfilled an important role in providing support, congenial entertainment and sport for a transitory expatriate community, especially on upcountry stations.

There are a number of designations for District Officers. I was appointed first as a District Officer (Cadet) and later on confirmation, became a District Officer. In practice in Uganda we were called Administrative Officers and, collectively and sometimes pejoratively, Admin. Appointments in the provincial administration – i.e. those working outside the central secretariat/ministries – were to Provincial Commissioner (PC) (Resident in Buganda), District Commissioner (DC) and Assistant District Commissioner (ADC). In my first district I began as ADC5, the most junior; by the end of the tour I was, temporarily, ADC1. I have also explained in the text the meaning of words in common use in Uganda which may not be clear to many readers.

Chapter 1

Family Background

My father's family had until the second half of the nineteenth century occupied a considerable amount of land in north Nottinghamshire around Mattersey and Lound, which, as far as I can discover, they lost thanks to a combination of incompetence and the agricultural slump towards the end of the century. My father, Reginald Plumer Walker, was born in London on 28 February 1891. His father, Plumer Cosby Walker, was then working for the Great Northern Railway, and the family lived in a modest house in Hornsey. Later my grandfather was transferred to Leeds on promotion to District Agent. In 1901 he became the Divisional Superintendent in Leeds.

My father's education was at Leeds Institute: Boys Modern School, then in the centre of Leeds. Later, in 1931, it moved to Lawnswood, and in 1972 on amalgamation with the girls school became Lawnswood High School. He left at seventeen in 1908. His headmaster, W. H. Barber, in a reference, stated that he was working at a level to matriculate for university, but I assume the family finances did not allow this course for the third son of a family where all the brothers (they had one sister, Nellie (Florence Ellen), who died in the flu epidemic of 1918) were expected to acquire professional rather than academic qualifications.

I also wonder if the state of relations between my grandfather, who according to my father was not an easy man, and his sons may have encouraged them to leave home as soon as they could. My uncle, Cyril Walker, told his son Brian that our grandfather was a shouting bully who terrified his secretary. What is certain is that the sons never forgave their father for marrying again in 1918 after the death in 1911 of their mother, his first wife, Mary Bustard. Only my father attended the wedding, as best man to his father. My grandfather retired with his second wife, Gertrude Thrippleton, to Bridlington, where he died in 1925. He is buried in Lawnswood Cemetery, Leeds, with his first wife, his daughter Nellie and four-day-old Margaret Plumer Walker, a daughter of the second marriage, who died in May 1920. This marriage also produced a son, Richard, whom I met only once in 1938 when I was six and he sixteen. According to the family he became a solicitor, practising for a time in Southport, but attempts to find him have failed. He, I assume, inherited most of the family papers.

The eldest brother was W(illiam) C(osby) Walker, known as 'Lavatory' Walker. He was an engineer who worked on the railways in South America. At the age of about forty he retired and returned to England. His marriage collapsed and he decided to live off his brothers, mainly Cyril and to a lesser extent my father, sending them the bills for his purchases, especially clothes. He remained in Falmouth until his death. Cyril worked for a short time as a trainee surveyor for the Great Northern Railway, moved into local government and ended as Valuer to the London County Council. During the Great War he became a captain in the Norfolk Regiment and before the end of the war married Mollie Hirsch, from a German family. It was typical of him that he was not deterred by her background at that time. Herbert Walker was an electrical engineer; I saw little of him. Jack, the youngest, was in the RAF at the end of the Great War and went to South Africa to run an orange farm bought with help from Cyril and my father. Jack was not sharp and omitted to discover if the farm had a regular water supply; the enterprise did not last long and he then

Plumer Cosby Walker, my grandfather

Florence Ellen Walker, my father's sister

worked in gold mines for the rest of his career. He married a South African whom we knew as Beryl 'the Boer'. They had no children.

I used to think that my father was a Victorian in his outlook but more recently I have come to the conclusion that the 'Victorian' elements in his character were in fact a Walker inheritance, because I have seen similar traits in my uncles, especially Cyril, and the cousins of my generation. Certainly, his assumption of responsibility for all family business matters was characteristic. My mother had no part in them until my father's death. He paid her a monthly allowance to cover both the household expenses and her own purchases, such as clothes. She always enjoyed having new clothes. During the Second World War in Kenya, she would buy material and make dresses. She would also knit dresses in unusual wools and when bored by them, unpick the wool, wash it and knit another to a different pattern. My impression is that my father only talked to her about financial matters when money became short towards the end of his life or when he thought her demands were unreasonable. The failure of the government to increase pensions from the time of his retirement until after his death caused real problems and he took a part time job.

Once, in Nairobi when I was ten or eleven, she was in the sitting room and burst into tears, complaining that my father was mean and did not give her enough to buy decent dresses. I was distressed and tried to comfort her. Now I suspect that this conflict over her allowance recurred over the years. She loved buying clothes, and a characteristic episode occurred during our home leave from Uganda in 1959. My parents had retired to Alderney in 1948. There was a good dress shop in Victoria Street in St Anne's. My mother had found two attractive dresses but told Susan and me that she was short of money so the dresses were impossible. We offered to buy one for her. She accepted with great pleasure and then said that after all she would buy the second. She asked us 'not to tell Reggie'. She wore the dress we had given and hid the other in her wardrobe. A month or so later she put it on, and when my father asked about it said that she had had it for some time. After my father's death in 1962, even when my mother's pension was pitiful, she made clear that she was not going to lower her standard of living. To make ends meet she sold jewellery and silver, so that when Susan and I went to Alderney to clear up after her death in 1965 many pieces which I remembered from my childhood had disappeared.

My father was not a natural communicator and found it difficult to express his inner feelings. His upbringing must have been partly responsible but there is in Walkers a tendency to arrive at a decision and, without talking much about it, to carry it through. I have seen this in myself. The result is that some course of action considered over a length of time and therefore familiar to oneself comes as a surprise to others, who could only conclude that it was a new idea pursued on the spur of the moment. The situation was not helped by my mother's detachment. This made her an entertaining and amusing companion with a dry way but did not encourage my father to talk easily to her about anything but the trivia of life. Just occasionally my father would lift the lid on himself and reveal a most surprising side of his personality and interests. Once we were, all three of us, listening to a Shakespeare play on the radio; I cannot now remember which one. My father began to speak with the actors and clearly recalled large sections of the play verbatim. When I showed my surprise he turned me away with a dismissive remark. I also remember his reading Rex Warner's *The Aerodrome* in short time and putting it down with the remark 'lavatory pan literature'.

He was a man of complete rectitude and high moral sense. A churchman all his life, he was an elder of St Andrew's Presbyterian church in Nairobi and a church warden in St Anne's in Alderney. He was, basically, middle to low church; my mother high. In Nairobi she did not attend St Andrew's but went occasionally to the Anglican cathedral not far from our house. She did worship in St Anne's but was sympathetic to the Catholic church on the Braye Road which lay below the garden of Les Rocquettes, our house at the foot of Victoria Street in St Anne's. All his life he took on voluntary work. Some, such as his involvement in staff clubs in both Malaya and Kenya, sprang from his work. Others were accepted out of a sense of duty – obligation, if you like. In Nairobi he was a Rotarian and a senior member of St John's Ambulance. In Alderney he ran a youth club in the Methodist Hall (I remember my sinking heart when he asked me to help set up the club equipment) and was treasurer and a moving influence in the appeal for a new hospital building for the Mignot Memorial Hospital, where both he and my mother died.

After retirement he became involved in local politics, being elected on the second attempt, to the States, the island's parliament. He became responsible for the island's finances and was eventually Vice-President of the States of Alderney and the island's representative on the States of Guernsey, to which Alderney was at that time linked. At the same time he was always busy about the house as well as working in the garden, difficult at Chateau L'Etoc, our first home close against the sea, but much better at Les Rocquettes with its walled garden full of gladioli in their many colours.

My father had a number of pet phrases or mannerisms of speech. To avoid swearing he would use 'bally', as in 'He is a bally fool'. He also 'exercised his mind'. My mother's favourite, which she used as long as I can remember, was 'I'll believe you; thousands wouldn't' (with an amused look).

My mother, Gladys Rabone, was born on 26 March 1896 at 122 Oldfield Road, Balsall Heath, Birmingham. Her father was Clement William Rabone, a master grocer; her mother was Lydia Argent. He was a handsome man and, from various remarks over the years, was probably a bit of a 'ladies' man'. There are pictures of my grandmother touring with my parents in 1932 and holding me as a baby. She died in Lapworth in 1947 at the age of eighty-one. When we were staying with the Harrises, cousins of my mother who lived in Hall Green, my mother and I would take the train to Lapworth to visit her. She lived with another old lady in a house just across the canal locks. I do not know where my mother went to school but assume it was the local schools. She obviously had a good education and was a tremendous reader all her life.

My impression from remarks she made from time to time was that she worked in a hospital before beginning her training as a nurse in the Guest Hospital, Dudley, in November 1917, when she was twenty-one. Her habit of heavy smoking, which led to the lung and liver cancer from which she died, began then. Nurses had to scrub floors and clean: smoking concealed the often disagreeable smells. Smoking fifty to sixty cigarettes a day for, in the end, almost fifty years caused

My mother as District Nurse

violent and convulsive coughing fits which alarmed those who did not
know her well. They could not understand why members of her family
did nothing to help. Another result was to make all the furnishings
and curtains stink of cigarette smoke. She qualified in November 1921

and then worked as District Nurse in the Evesham area, living at Badsey. From 1923 to 1924 she trained in fever and fever nursing in the North Eastern Fever Hospital; in 1924 she qualified as a midwife at the Maternity Hospital in Birmingham; and in 1925 she obtained her Certificate in Tuberculosis in the Royal Chest Hospital in City Road, EC1. She went to Malaya in 1926.

My mother had very good taste in her clothes and in interior design. One of her early interests, shared with a friend in Evesham, was Ruskin ware, now highly collectable. I still have her collection and some pieces bequeathed to me by her friend, Lucy Chambers. My mother's letters were the same as her speech, dry and amused, so one could hear her voice in her writing. A characteristic picture of her in Alderney was of her seated on a sitting room chair with a book open on its broad arm, knitting, occasionally counting the stitches (she did not need to look at her knitting because she was so skilled) and watching TV. She would, of course, be smoking. Her drinks routine, started in the tropics, was a gin and lime at lunch time and a whisky or two with plenty of water in the evening.

She enjoyed music, particularly light operetta and musicals, and I remember her playing extracts from *Crest of the Wave* and *1066 – and All That* in our drawing room in Nairobi. The music from *Chu Chin Chow* in particular made her sentimental. She loved these shows and I have wondered if she had been to them with someone on whom she was keen. There is a photo of a young soldier taken during the Great War with, written on the back on 24 October 1917, 'With best wishes and lots of love, from yours Howard'. Who was he? Did he get killed? My mother never mentioned him.

My mother was very firm-minded, a quality which could make her implacable. Her brother, John, had emigrated to Australia just after the Great War. During the Second World War he joined the Australian forces, was captured by the Japanese in Singapore and sent to work on the Burma railway. The characteristics which he shared with my mother carried him through: determination and a firm conviction that Britain would win the war. After the Japanese surrender he bought, with his deferred pay, twelve acres in Helena Valley outside Perth. When their mother died, in 1947, John was convinced that my mother had inherited a considerable amount but was unwilling to share it with him. This was untrue and my mother did not forgive him for this accusation. Attempts by John to effect a reconciliation failed. In 1965, when my mother was dying of cancer, John visited the UK but again my mother refused to see him. John decided to fly to Alderney but arrived after my mother's death, so was not able to try yet again to make up their relationship. He was deeply distressed at her funeral, which in many ways was a dismal occasion. The rain poured down, and St Anne's parish church, a huge building constructed to hold a large proportion of the British army garrison of 5,000 that had manned the forts around Alderney until the 1920s, leaked, with the rain bouncing off her coffin into a metal bucket with a loud ping. We stood together in the rain by her grave.

Chapter 2

Malaya

My father joined the traffic department of the Great Northern Railway in King's Cross as a junior clerk in October 1908 and transferred to the accountant's office in May 1910. His time in London was spent taking his basic accountancy exams as an external student at the London School of Economics. He left to become a travelling auditor on the Federated Malay States (FMS) Railways, to which he was appointed on 7 March 1914.

My father joined the Malay States Volunteer Rifles (MSVR) and was soon involved in active service. The start of the Great War was followed shortly after by a rebellion, the Singapore Mutiny. A battalion of the Indian 5th Light Infantry, which was made up of Pathans and Rajputs, mutinied on 15 February 1915. In the absence of British army units, which had been recalled to the Western Front, the battalion was responsible for the protection of Singapore. There were a number of reasons for the mutiny: friction within the battalion, the influence of local agitators and the belief that a coming posting to Hong Kong would be in fact to France or Mesopotamia. There had also been discontent in the Sikh battalion of the Malay States Guides caused by a posting to Singapore from the Guides' base in Taiping. The Sikh battalion was returned to Taiping before the mutiny.

A detachment from HMS *Cadmus* and the MSVR were the first to respond to the mutiny in Singapore. They were later reinforced by the arrival of the Shropshire Regiment and by French, Japanese and Russians from their warships in Singapore. The mutineers had hoped that the German POWs held on the island would escape and help them to seize Singapore. The POWs refused to help and the mutiny was soon over. The MSVR were ordered to carry out the shooting by firing squad of the thirty-seven mutineers condemned to death; was my father involved?

An early photograph album has pictures of my father in army uniform as a private in the Malay States Volunteer Rifles guarding government offices in Kuala Lumpur. The next photographs are in Singapore: the officers' mess of the 5th Light Infantry, described as the 'rallying point'; Normanton Barracks 'MSVR in occupation Feb 1915'; and officers' quarters 5th Light Infantry 'used for accommodation of MSVR Feb to March 1915'.

In April 1915 another rebellion, known as the Outbreak and led by To'langgut, took place in Kelantan. The reasons for the revolt are still debated. Although against the government, it was not a 'freedom' event but was influenced by changes in the tax system which affected both landowners and farmers. It was soon suppressed with help from the Malay Volunteers and a company of the Shropshire Light Infantry. A photograph shows that my father went on SS *Calypso* to Kelantan with the Penang Malay Volunteers 'to assist quell native rising'. In June 1916 he was at the MSVR training camp in Taiping. There is a photograph of a group of Volunteers, one of whom, Norris, was killed in action and another, Captain Green, was wounded (presumably in Malaya rather than elsewhere). My father never mentioned this fighting.

Later he moved to Tumpat, where he returned to his job on the FMS Railways. There are pictures of Tumpat station and wharf, Kuala Krau resthouse, Gemas station, Samantan village and the river Kuala Lebin. Among the pictures is the first of my father in civilian dress – whites – outside his bungalow. The album ends with pictures of floods in Kuala Lumpur.

In a letter to the commandant of the Kenya Defence Force on 8 January 1936, the commandant of the FMS Volunteer Force stated that my father had served with the MSVR from 7 July 1914 to 31 December 1920 and then in the Malay States Volunteer Regiment from 1 January 1921 to 31 August 1935. When he resigned, the hon

My father outside his bungalow

secretary of the mess wrote thanking him for 'the work and time he had devoted to the interests of the mess'. He continued shooting and we have silver spoons he won as prizes.

My father's record of service in the FMS Railways shows that he was confirmed in his appointment on 8 April 1917 and made an assistant accountant on 1 January 1918, when he may have moved to Kuala Lumpur. For a month in 1922 he was seconded to the public works department as a financial officer; acted as deputy accountant – i.e. number two in the department – from 22 September 1922 to 6 February 1924; and was made deputy accountant on 29 January 1926, just before his thirty-fifth birthday. He acted as chief accountant on three occasions, in 1926/27, 1930 and 1934/35. In 1930 the general manager, J. Strachen, wrote to say he had been 'thoroughly satisfied' with his work as acting chief accountant. Somehow this progression in his career was typical of my father, steady and effective, moving from a junior official in 1914 to second in the department in fourteen years. He was careful and conscientious.

Was that all my father was? The recollections of friends from his Malayan days reveal another side to his personality.

Until he married in 1927 my father led the typical life of a bachelor in Malaya. He was known there as Plumer Walker, in Kenya as Reggie. When he arrived in Malaya and was posted upcountry he had lived with 'Old Man' Hyam, who worked in the FMS Railways. Later he had stayed with Hyam in the Seven Dials area of Kuala Lumpur when going and returning from leave. Hyam was the father of Cecily Beith, a friend of my parents in Malaya, and by one of those happy chances of life the grandfather of Rob Beith, my best man, with whom I shared a bedroom when we both arrived for our first term at King's School, Canterbury, then evacuated to the Carlyon Bay Hotel near St Austell in Cornwall.

He was a member of the Selangor club, and there are pictures of him, after his marriage, in formal and fancy dress at club dances. He was also a devoted Mason throughout his life, as my grandfather had been. Being a Mason was important in career terms in Malaya. He continued as a Mason in Kenya and I remember my mother going to ladies' nights. After retirement to Alderney he was a member of the Guernsey Lodge and had ordered a new apron just before he died. My mother sent it back and demanded a refund, which they gave with great reluctance. My father was not an obsessive Mason. While I was at Oxford he asked if I would like to become one. I declined, because I am at heart a non-joiner, but also because the secrecy about its activities made me uneasy.

Cecily Beith described my father as amusing, a great talker and fond of dances. In Nairobi I remember my mother saying after an evening out that my father had had the party 'in stitches'. When I looked surprised, she said he could be most amusing. In Kuala Lumpur he had a red two-seater sports car. Again by one of those chances of life, Ivy Wright, a friend of the Hastings, was invited to Susan's and my wedding and recognised my father as an old flame not seen since he left Malaya. She remembered him driving her in his red sports car.

He became a member of the flying club – there are aerial photographs of Kuala Lumpur taken during his flights – though whether he enjoyed flying is doubtful, because he told me that he was always sick in the air. He was a left-handed tennis player and in Kenya we played each other until I was sixteen (and he fifty-six). He was not much interested in the more commonly pursued games such as golf, polo and bridge. Both he and my mother preferred mahjong, which they continued to play regularly with friends in Nairobi on a Thursday night. In Kenya he gave me his golf clubs so I could learn but they were elderly even then and far from a full set. The impression is that he had a group of friends with whom he went on local leave, often to Port Dickson, where the Railways had holiday bungalows. Not all his recreations were physical. He spoke Malay and helped to test railway staff taking their language examinations.

The question is: where did his girlfriends come from? According to Cecily Beith, a Railway colleague, R. H. Bilke, tried without success to interest my father in one of his daughters. He certainly knew a number of Nursing Sisters, who were given membership of the

The sports car

Selangor Club. How close he was to any one of them is, again, not clear. The fact that he surprised my mother when he proposed to her suggests that he had gone out with a group and had then decided that my mother was the one. They married on 17 November 1927 in St Andrew's Presbyterian church in Kuala Lumpur, where the minister was R. (Roy) D. Whitehorn. Later Whitehorn became professor of Church History and then President of Westminster College,

Railway offices, Kuala Lumpur

Cambridge, and was my guardian when I was at King's and my parents still in Kenya. Their honeymoon was in Brastagi in Sumatra. Photographs show them riding and my mother, surprisingly, playing golf.

My parents lived in a house on Sayers Road. In 1989, when I was attending a Commonwealth Security Conference in Kuala Lumpur, Susan and I were lent a car and driver to look for both her and my parents' houses. Both still stand. The Hastings' house is now part of the French Embassy. Susan's father, an advocate in Kuala Lumpur, founded the firm of Lovelace and Hastings, which still exists. My parents' house still belongs to the Railways and was occupied by a French technical aid worker. His wife had just returned to France, so that, when we had identified the house from photos and – accompanied by a friend in the British High Commission – knocked on the door, he received us with pleasure and entertained us. He obviously saw our arrival as a desirable interruption of the chess game he was playing against himself. The interior of the house looked unchanged since before the Second

My parents' wedding, 1927

World War; the electricity arrangements certainly appeared original. The final pleasure was sitting with drinks in the room over the porch which was my playroom and which features in the only memory from my three years in Malaya: of pushing a large – to me, then – red train engine.

Impressions of their life in Sayers Road come almost exclusively from photos: neat servants, a fox terrier called Chippy, two cars with the sais (driver), a tidy garden. There was, of course, no air-conditioning at that time, so my father would return for lunch and a complete change of 'ducks', the white suit in which he worked.

My father was active in a number of social and benevolent clubs. He was president of the United Railway Employees Benefit Society, a post he took over in May 1926 from Bilke after his death. The formal address given to him on 28 January 1935 by the junior officers in the accounts department lists his voluntary activities 'great and small, such as the St Andrew's Presbyterian Church as member of the Board of Managers, Secretary, Treasurer and member of Session, Royal Society of St George, Toc H, Kuala Lumpur Wing, Young Men's Christian Association from time to

The family and cars in Sayers Road – my playroom over the porch

time on Board, United Railway Employees' Benefit Society, FMS as President...'.

On her marriage my mother gave up working, but during the Second World War in Kenya she returned to nursing at the Maia Carbery Nursing Home in Nairobi, which was used for servicemen.

I had always assumed that I was their only baby. However, later in life my mother told me once that an older brother had been still-born. It must have been a great disappointment, not just personally but because my father loved children and was good at communicating with them. When I was born, on 25 February 1932, my father was forty-one and my mother in her late thirties, old at that time for having children. Bungsai Hospital, where I was born, was still standing in 1989 but about to be demolished. Even the newer buildings were old, and its use by the Japanese during the Second World War as an interrogation centre had given people a dislike of the place.

My baptism took place in the Presbyterian Church of England in York on 9 August 1932, when my parents were on leave. Roy Whitehorn was again involved. This was the first in a series of baptisms and confirmations which took place over some thirty years. At the time they had a kind of logic, even if some appeared unnecessary. In retrospect they become slightly comic though, in themselves, serious events. At the age of sixteen, while at King's School Canterbury, I was confirmed in Canterbury Cathedral by Archbishop Fisher. At King's I had met Brother Peter of the Anglican Franciscans. His character and gentle persuasiveness made a great impression. The result was a visit to the order's house outside Cerne Abbas in Dorset. I became a Companion of St Francis on 11 February 1952 during my first year at Oxford and developed an admiration and veneration for St Francis which has lasted throughout my life. My contact with the Franciscans diminished during my second and third years at Oxford. If I went to church it was usually in Trinity Chapel. At home in Alderney I went with my parents to the parish church of St Anne's.

At the end of Oxford I started to go to the Cowley Fathers on the Iffley Road. At about the same time I met Susan Hastings, a Roman

Catholic. After we married in April 1955 and I had started the First Devonshire Course in October the same year, we continued the pattern: she to a Catholic church, Greyfriars on the Iffley Road, me to the Cowley Fathers, both being near the flat we occupied in her mother's house at 186 Iffley Road. In Uganda we both went to the Catholic Mass in the Goan Institute in Soroti. By the beginning of 1957 I had decided to become a Catholic, and my reception took place in the little chapel in the convent of the Franciscan Sisters at the mission at Madera outside Soroti. The Convent, now in dire need of repair, still stands and the chapel is in the same place. Bishop Greif, the Bishop of Tororo, officiated. He was a Tyrolian Mill Hill Father, a dear man whose spluttered English was almost incomprehensible. He was recognised by his VW 'Beetle'. The saying of Sir Andrew Cohen, the governor of Uganda, was: 'Tarantino (the Verona Fathers Bishop of Gulu) for a beano; Greif for life.'

On 2 March 1957 Susan and I sat at the back of the chapel with the nuns in the front. Greif was unsure whether he had to baptise me but was persuaded just to receive my request for forgiveness and the declaration of my wish to join the Roman Catholic Church. Greif then confirmed me – my second. At the end of the ceremony he called Susan forward and asked for her wedding ring. She thought he was about to marry us again. However, he just wished to bless the ring, and then gave us the wedding prayer and blessing: 'and let her ever follow the pattern of holy women: let her be dear to her husband like Rachel; wise like Rebecca; long-lived and faithful like Sara…that you may see your children's children even to the third and fourth generation…' We already had one child and went on to have two more and nine grandchildren.

When I joined the Security Service, on the last day of 1962, we had bought a house in East Sheen. Our parish was St Mary Magdalen, Mortlake; Monseignor Gibney, the vicar general of Southwark archdiocese, our parish priest. We joined a parish discussion group under the mild and slightly worried guidance of the curate, Father Nolan. During the course of a discussion I disclosed my chequered

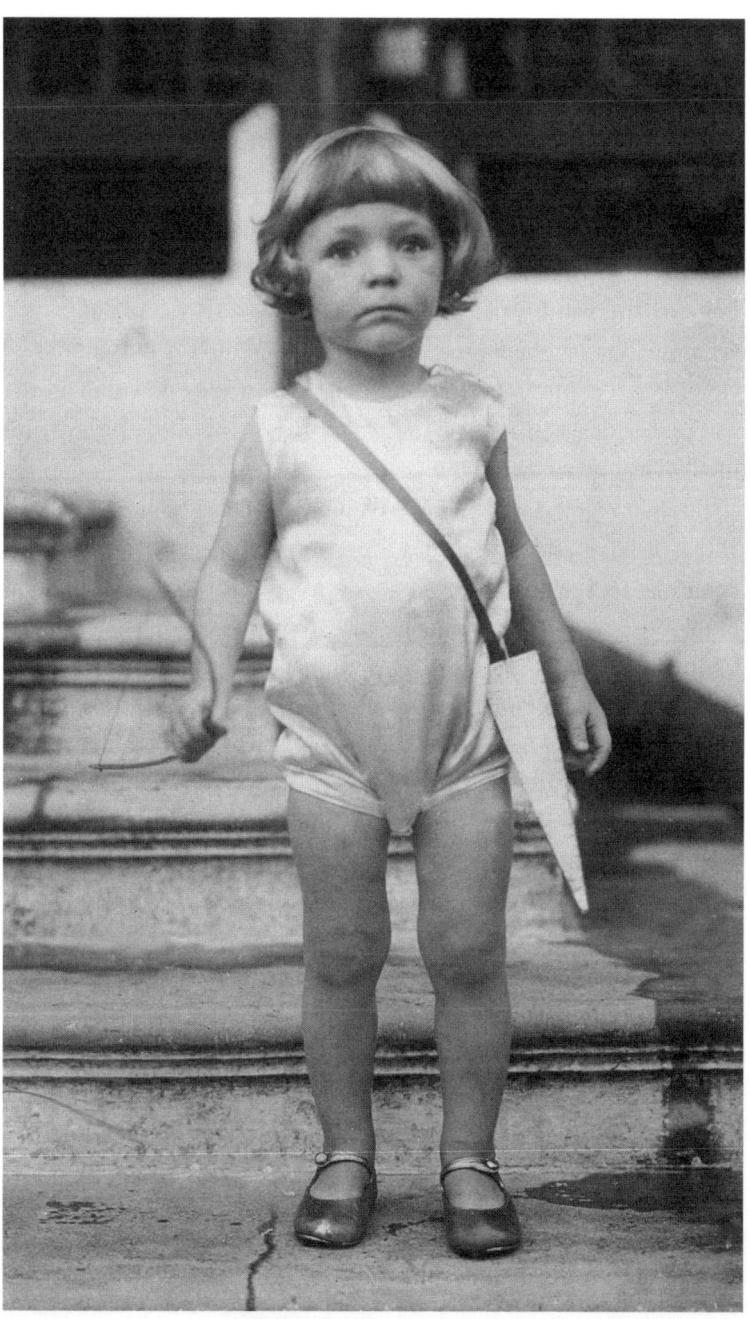

My third birthday, dressed as Cupid

church history. Father Nolan began to agonise. Had I been properly baptised? If not, was the confirmation in Madera valid? Could I take the risk? He recommended another baptism and confirmation. I should, of course, have refused, and nowadays the point would not even be made by a Catholic priest. But there was no baptism certificate available – it turned up after my parents' deaths – and one has to remember what the pre-Vatican II Catholic Church was like. So I agreed and was baptised, in a basin in the sacristy, and confirmed yet again. So how should my two baptisms and three confirmations be viewed; as a climb to ever greater heights or a slide downhill all the way? In clerical terms the latter was true – archbishop, bishop and finally vicar general.

I do not regret my time in the Church of England, for which I had and still have affection and admiration for some of its features, especially its music. However, at my reception I felt I was coming home, and, except in moments of extreme exasperation with the Church authorities or a parish priest, have felt no urge to return to the Church of England. On the other hand, I have no inhibition in receiving communion from a Church of England priest who clearly shares the Roman Catholic belief in the nature of the Eucharist.

To return to Malaya after my baptism. I have mentioned the only memory of the three years there: pushing a red train engine across the floor of my playroom above the porch of the house in Sayers Road. The rest has to be constructed from photographs. These show me swimming in the enclosure at Port Dickson, with my parents outside the house, at parties. The least attractive pictures are of me dressed as Cupid in a silk outfit with wings at a fancy dress party at the Selangor Club for my third birthday. I suspect, strongly, that I was very spoilt.

Chapter 3

Kenya Childhood

In 1935 my father was appointed Chief Accountant of the Kenya and Uganda Railways and Harbours (KUR&H). The move to Nairobi was preceded by leave in the UK. At the end of leave the Union Castle ship the *Llandaff Castle*, taking my parents to Mombasa, left England on 9 August 1935. (The *Llandaff Castle* was torpedoed and sunk off the South African coast in 1942.) During the voyage they met (Ethel) Rita (Le Breton) Thompson.

Rita Thompson, a member of a Jersey family, had been born on 9 May 1900 in Kensington, and was educated at the Froebel Education Institute in Kensington and then at Godolphin and Latymer. She claimed Lily Langtry, the 'Jersey Lily', as a cousin. On the *Llandaff Castle* she was escorting a little girl of six to Cape Town. Unsettled in London after her mother's death and the marriage of her sister, and with an interest in Africa, she hoped to find a job in South Africa either with children or in an office. In her youth she had taught for five years in the Froebel school, she could teach music and she was also a trained secretary.

During the voyage a friendship developed between my parents and Miss Thompson. At the same time, she and I took a shine to each other. The result was an invitation to her to become my nursery governess, which she accepted. She then became a large element in my life, even though she left us in April 1938, when my parents and I went on home leave, to become my father's secretary and supervisor of the typing pool in the accounts department in Railway headquarters in Nairobi.

Rita Thompson

Her task until I was about to go to my prep school, Kenton College, was, essentially, to look after me during the day, except for the period after lunch, when I was expected to rest. In the morning, if I woke before my parents, I would go into their bedroom and lie on the floor wrapped in an eiderdown. Miss Thompson would then prepare me for breakfast, which took place on the upstairs verandah, an area enclosed with windows looking north-east across Nairobi to Mount Kenya and Ol Doinyo Sabuk. It was one of my early pleasures to see Mount Kenya in the early morning with snow on the peaks. At this time the far end of the verandah was my play area, full of soft toys, cushions and rugs with which I constructed houses and began to play the games of imagination with which only children entertained themselves.

During the morning I was taught to read and write, and also the beginnings of piano. On my fifth birthday Miss Thompson gave me a fountain pen; I was really growing up. Of her lessons nothing remains, except for a vague memory of using one of the copybooks which were then common. What I do recall were the evenings, which began with a soak in the large free-standing bath. She would read to me, and it was my idea of bliss to lie in the warm water and listen to the *Just William* stories.

She continued to be close to my parents in Nairobi, usually spending local leaves with us. In 1939, when war was declared, we were all together at Lawford's Hotel in Malindi. After leaving us, she lived at first in a flat in the centre of Nairobi, and then at Plum's Hotel, long since disappeared, on Sclaters Road. Thin and spinsterish, with her hair tied in a bun at the back of her head, she nevertheless always made a great impression on men. I suppose that her obvious competence appealed to them and the wives saw her as no threat. Her fussiness did cause difficulties though, and an attempt to settle with my parents in Alderney after her retirement in 1956 sadly resulted in disaster. My mother in particular found her tiresome. A move to Glasgow to be near her sister was more successful and she worked for years for the Professor of Forensic Medicine at the university. We kept in touch until her death in 1987 in Scarborough.

My parents' house for most of their time in Nairobi was No. 1 Ngong Road. Its style was typical of the senior Railway staff houses of the 1930s, and, indeed, of many other houses in Kenya of the same period: rusticated stone. Across Ngong Road was a similar house occupied by Blin Stoyle, the chief mechanical engineer, a large and immensely fat man much addicted to horse racing and drinking. Beyond him was a house occupied by Alfred Dalton, the Superintendent of the Line and Deputy General Manager to Sir Reginald Robins, from whom he took over as general manager.

By the front door was an open verandah covered with tropical plants in pots. In the hall a door on the left opened into the sitting room and another on the right into the dining room, with the scullery, locked larder and kitchen beyond. At the back of the hall was my father's study, which I remember for the large poinsettia bush outside its window. Upstairs were three bedrooms, a dressing room used by my father off my parents' bedroom, a bathroom and a loo. The most attractive room was the enclosed verandah; its only defect was green paint which, to the irritation of my father, never quite dried.

No. 1 Ngong Road

In front of the house, towards Nairobi, was an open uncut field, used for games with my friends. Beyond the field was the old Secretariat, an old colonial building of wood and corrugated iron. It burnt down one night just before the Second World War. I remember looking at the skeleton of the building the next day.

The back gate of the drive, which we never used, opened onto First Ngong Avenue, a quiet road lined with jacaranda trees. The same side of the avenue as us was occupied by other Railway houses. The drive leading to the back gate was lined with spiky euphorbia and rose bushes, and was the scene of one of my crashes when learning to ride a bicycle given as a birthday present. A failure to turn properly ended in a dive into the middle of a rose bush, from which I needed both parents to extricate me. Beyond the kitchen was a banda (an open building with wooden posts and a thatched roof) in which my mother's Vauxhall 10 was housed. It had been collected in 1938 from the factory in Birmingham and was used by my mother throughout the war. One night an attempt was made to steal it. On this occasion its main defect, being a bad starter, saved us. Miss Thompson was staying in her usual room at the back of the house and alerted my father, who went out but failed to catch the thief.

Next to the banda was a tall fir tree. Near its top the trunk was cut off and a tree house platform installed. It was a most agreeable place to which to retire even if a sticky climb.

At the front of the house and to the left was the garage, also in rusticated stone. The first car I remember was a buff-coloured 1936 Dodge with a ram on the bonnet. Its headlights stuck out from the sides of the bonnet like eyes on stalks. As a treat when we had gone for a drive on the plains, now the Nairobi National Park, I would be allowed to sit between the headlight stalk and the mudguard. My father would make sure I was tightly wedged in and then drive the car slowly. It was an exhilarating experience.

The roads in Kenya in the 1930s and 1940s were mostly graded murram. In the areas of black cotton soil they became gluey in the rains. My father, a careful driver, would go at little more than 40 mph in these conditions. Driving to Mombasa required a stay overnight in Kajiado. In 1962 Susan and I drove from Nairobi to Mombasa on the direct road in six hours.

Behind the garage were the servants' quarters. The open drain from their washhouse ran through the garden to the open field. This was where I played with my lead models, especially cars and lorries, because the damp ground in a frequently dry and dusty garden allowed me to make roads, buildings and battle scenes. The games were mostly war-orientated; inevitably during the Second World War boys wanted to have models of soldiers, army vehicles, warships and planes. The conditions would appal people today in this cleanliness-obsessed world. It was, however, a most satisfactory place to play.

Later my father acquired an old guards van, which was mounted on blocks beside the garage. My electric train set, a Trix bought from Bassett Lowke in Holborn in 1938 during home leave and supplemented in Nairobi by more carriages and engines, was laid out on a board at the end. As a boy I was used to entertaining myself and spent many hours happily making wooden tanks and planes in the van. We had retained its kennel at one end for transporting dogs. It was large enough for an adult to crawl in. I was told that in a moment of foolishness my father was persuaded to climb in by Derek and Bruce Sinclair, the sons of a coffee planter in Kabete. They locked the door and turned the hose on him through the ventilation holes. He was let out eventually, soaked!

My parents brought their wire-haired terrier from Malaya but he must have died soon afterwards, as I do not remember him. I do remember clearly our two Sealyhams, Punch and Judy, a brother and sister, who produced Patch. My mother had a regular weekly routine of de-ticking them. The large grey ticks, full of blood, would be removed, placed in an ashtray and popped with her inevitable cigarette. When the Sealyhams died my parents acquired a Scottie, Wallace.

The cats were my particular joy. We began with Tinker Bell, who produced a large tabby, Twinkle. He was my cat; immensely affectionate, he would put a paw each side of my neck, and butt and rub my face. He also had the remarkable trick of begging for food by sitting upright on his haunches, putting his front paws together and moving them up and down in a gesture of supplication. We had no idea where he could have acquired this skill.

Perhaps the most remarkable cat was John, who adopted us not long after we arrived in Nairobi. We did not know his age but worked out that he must have been nearing twenty when he died. It was my parents' custom to put our animals into kennels when we went on leave. They were run by a remarkable old lady, Mrs Mallett, at her house on the Thika Road beyond Mathari Mental Hospital. She also kept civet cats in cages. In 1942, when we were going to South Africa, we arranged to take the animals to Mrs Mallett the day before we left. When the time came John had disappeared and a search of his usual haunts failed to reveal him. So he had to be left. Three months later we returned, and the afternoon of our return were standing in the garden when John, in perfect health, walked up the drive and rolled in front of us. How did he know we were going away? Was it the atmosphere, the unusual activity? Had he been watching each day for our return?

In 1962 No. 1 was still standing and occupied. By the 1990s it had been demolished, and the whole area is now covered with tower blocks occupied by government departments.

Kenya was subject to periodic locust plagues. During the war, when locust eradication was less effective, the swarms reached Nairobi. The houseboys (as our servants were then called) would rush out banging saucepans and dustbin lids to try, usually unsuccessfully, to drive them out of the garden. They would also catch some for eating. It was the sheer mass of the swarms which impressed me. It was also disagreeable to have locusts crashing into one.

Towards the end of the war a line of stores were set up on the plains selling surplus military equipment. They were the place to go when building a simple radio set or when one wanted construction materials. On one occasion I agreed to take our two Sealyhams for a walk and went down the hill onto the plains towards the stores. It did, of course, take much longer than I had expected. By the time I got home it was almost dark and the dogs were exhausted. My mother, who had been onto the police to report my failure to return, was furious. The more usual walk with the dogs was along Kilamanjaro Avenue, where I always hoped to be able to look across the plains to see snow on the mountain. Part of the entertainment during such walks was to count how many times the dogs would lift their legs.

Looking back, especially after working in Uganda, I realise how little contact I had with black Kenyans. I knew the servants and their families, who stayed in the servants' quarters from time to time. Africans as a whole formed part of the background, an interesting and agreeable one, but one which made no direct impact. I lived in a 'white' environment both at home and at school. My father had more contact, but even in the Railways it would have been restricted, because the middle and senior ranks were mostly white or Asian. This situation sprang partly from the circumstances of colonial rule and partly from the fact that the Uganda railway was constructed for the most part by labour from India, some making a career in the Railways and others staying on and developing businesses, usually shops ('dukas').

THE KENYA AND UGANDA RAILWAYS AND HARBOURS

My father's office was on the ground floor of the Railway headquarters, just to the left of the main entrance portico. The offices were another building in rusticated stone, which enabled me to climb into his office through the window. His work on the Railways was a constant background to our life. Many of his friends were in the Railways. One family I remember well: the Kirklands, who lived in an older colonial house on Lower Hill Road. Kirkland was the locomotive superintendent. My particular friend was his son, David. The two daughters continued to be involved with our family: Gwenda married John Lane, the son of a railway official, who went into the army;

The 1936 Dodge outside the Nairobi Club

Dorothy married Bernard Sheldon, who was first in the Malayan civil service and later Legal Advisor in the Security Service. Again by life's chance, Bernard was offered a job in Susan's father's office in Kuala Lumpur. It was at the Kirklands' house that I was offered my first cigarette, if you could call it that, made from grass rolled in canna leaves. It was disgusting. Perhaps that experience reinforced my loathing of the cigarette smoke that I always associated with my mother. Indeed, one of my first memories is of climbing up onto a sofa beside her and getting the smoke from her cigarette in my eyes.

Children's parties took place at the Railway club at the foot of Whitehouse Road. Such golf as I acquired was on the railway golf course, with its 'browns' (carefully rolled sand instead of grass). As in Malaya, my father was involved in staff clubs. I remember going, with reluctance, to a party in the club for Asian staff, of which he was president. The boredom of sitting on a chair against a side wall, with no idea of what I was supposed to be doing, was excruciating. Later in Uganda I recognised this style of party in Indian homes or offices. Seats were placed around the wall. The Indian wives attended but for the most part were silent. The men talked while Susan and I ate hot curry nibbles and drank either very strong whisky or sweet, sometimes saffron, tea. They were not easy occasions. It was much easier to chat informally with the traders and cotton ginnery owners about their businesses. The main voluntary work of my father was St John's Ambulance. He was the senior official in charge of the railway

My father in his office in Nairobi

The private carriage at Athi River 1948

unit and his work for the brigade earned him appointment as a Commander Brother of the Order of St John. In 1948, when he was retiring, there was a presentation ceremony at which Sir Godfrey Rhodes, a former General Manager, handed him a clock. It was one of the first of such occasions I found interesting. Perhaps at sixteen I was beginning to grow up.

My father was a mild man but I became aware of one episode of office politics which angered him. He discovered a loose note in a file which showed that a group, including a family friend, were trying to undermine his position. He threatened that if they did not stop he would go to the Colonial Secretary. My father must have been very angry to make such a threat.

Being senior in the Railways had some advantages. The best, for me, was a private carriage when he was visiting parts of the railway away from Nairobi. About a quarter of the carriage, at one end, was a sitting room with windows on three sides and, between padded benches, a table on which meals were served. Next door were the bedrooms, similar to those on the sleepers; then a bathroom and loo; and finally the kitchen and servants' accommodation. Between stopping points we would play card or board games. I can remember throwing the pieces of a Monopoly game about when I was losing badly!

During the war my father was a Brigadier in the Kenya Regiment, I think by virtue of having to organise the transportation of military material and his long involvement in the army reserves. He attended courses and exercises. Once the Italian campaign was over, his responsibilities were not demanding. Then the nearest the war came was in the Indian Ocean, where Japanese submarines continued to sink ships. Rita Thompson saw wreckage from a sunken ship as she was going to India on leave in 1942.

In 1945 and again in 1947 my father went to Mauritius to examine and reorganise the Mauritius civil service. I have not been able to find any papers relating to these visits, but it is clear that he enjoyed them. He brought back small souvenirs: seashells, a phial containing the different layers of earth found in Mauritius (sadly soon broken) and a turtle shell, which still hangs on our kitchen wall today.

Chapter 4

Preparatory School (Kenton College)

In January 1939, still only six, I was sent as a boarder to Kenton College, a prep school in Nairobi. It was built, like our house, of rusticated stone. The headmaster, Finlay R. Cramb, was a co-founder of the school, which began in Kijabe and then moved to Nairobi. It is still on the same site in Nairobi but much expanded and most successful. In 1995 Susan and I went to Kenya to visit Cheshire Homes, and by a happy chance the chairman of Cheshire Kenya, Charles Gardner, was also a governor of Kenton, having been there himself. It was curious looking at the team shields to see my name. The headmaster had a strict policy of keeping the school one-third European, one-third African and one-third Asian.

As a very small boy moved from home to a completely new environment, I had to learn to survive on my own without constant affection. I was miserable and for many mornings cried quietly in my bed in the small dormitory for new arrivals. The only slight consolation was that other new boys were in the same condition. Looking back, I think the school tried to help. I remember walking on the terrace behind the school building being given raw carrots by the matron.

My first taste of school punishment came in my second term. My parents wished me to be taught the piano. My first term's report, from Mrs Barrow-Dowling, stated: 'A promising boy. Patrick has shown real interest in his lessons and has therefore made progress.' Despite this report Cramb gave me four strokes of the cane for failing to practise conscientiously. Friends from Kenton days told me later that Cramb liked beating (though he only beat me once again during my time at Kenton). It was, however, a curious way of encouraging a love of music. I remember rubbing my bum on an outside wall to remove the stinging. Later Mrs Barrow-Dowling left and I was taught by Raoul Prater, who was described as a 'Free Austrian'. He was a careful and kind teacher whom I remember mainly for the star branded on his forehead.

Encouraged by my mother's love of music and by the benign influence of my second school, King's School Canterbury, I developed a great love of music. However, at Kenton and during the holidays, when lessons continued under Mrs Barrow-Dowling, my recollections are of hoping for the best during lessons and enduring the half-hour practice each day on which my mother insisted. Practice at home took place on a Chappell 'baby' grand, brought from Malaya. Later it went to Alderney and then out to Uganda.

At the outbreak of the war the school moved to Westwood Park, a country hotel about eleven miles from Nairobi, beyond Dagoretti Corner. Unfortunately it is an army training centre and not open to the public, so I have not been able to visit it during recent trips to Kenya. The hotel looked over a lake formed by the damming of the river Mbagathi, from which a ram pumped water up to houses. On the other side of the river was the Karen estate, where the headmaster had a house. He occasionally took boys home, where his wife looked after us; I thought it most imposing. Not long after we arrived, the lake disappeared when the dam broke one night after heavy rain. Further out beyond the hotel was a farm on which a lion was shot – it had been attacking cattle. The event caused some excitement among the boys.

The hotel had been modified to make it more suitable for a school. The detached chalets at the rear of the main hotel became dormitories for the younger boys and classrooms. The verandahs at the front were enclosed to make dormitories, as was the lounge. After the first year or so I was moved into one of the larger dormitories, of which one end was open. This was the cause of some moments of terror. I was sure an animal could walk into the dormitory; indeed, it could. Night after night I heard what I was convinced was at least a leopard. In retrospect I think it was a nightjar. However, it must have been the cause of regular nightmares, in which I was hiding from a lion behind a sofa or just the other side of a window outside which the lion moved. This dormitory, with its corrugated iron roof, was also the cause of a sound which has given me pleasure all my life: rain falling on a metal roof. Later I went to a residential house halfway up the drive run by the second master, Jack Hastings. He was much given to having favourites; I was not one.

Assembly and services took place in a temporary building at the rear of the main hotel. The evening service on Sundays had a bittersweet flavour. It marked the end of a brief period of freedom to play, and the evening light could be seen through an open door. Certain hymns spark memories of that time: 'There is a green hill' and 'The day thou gavest Lord is ended'.

Westwood Park

The assembly hall was the scene of my first shock at a public event. Cramb came into hall with a solemn face. We stood around the walls waiting. He then announced the sinking of HMS *Hood*, a ship we all knew about. The hall was also where the headmaster criticised me publicly but obliquely. This arose out of a mass rejection of a particularly disgusting pudding. It was made out of ground maize and absolutely without taste. A group of boys, including myself, were complaining. I suddenly said that we should refuse to eat it. Staff concern followed and those supervising the meal spotted me as a ringleader. In assembly the headmaster, looking at me, spoke about boys trying to cause trouble. That was the end of the matter. Like much school food of that time, it was pretty unpleasant. Most of the time we just accepted it. We were, however, surprised by the arrival of plates of camel meat, of which herds were kept on the plains outside Nairobi.

SICKNESS

Sickness of one form or another seemed in retrospect to play a large part of life in Kenya and in Uganda later. I was generally regarded as a sickly boy, and picked up every passing infection. When tired at the end of the day at Kenton I would feel terrible and turn a green colour, and be sent to the sanatorium. A pill and a night's rest usually did the trick. I was also subject to large boils on my legs both before going to school and during school. At first it fell to Miss Thompson to poultice and then squeeze the heads, an excruciatingly painful process. A holiday in 1937 on a paddle steamer in Uganda was dominated by these wretched boils. Later, at Kenton, one batch below my knee involved placing my leg in a bucket of very hot water. When they eventually burst the product was enormous and gratifying. I still have the scars. After a bout of illness when I was about ten, a member of staff asked seriously if I liked being ill. I was surprised by the question and denied any such wish.

I had been vaccinated against smallpox and inoculated against typhoid and diphtheria and later against yellow fever, but in those days there were no inoculations against childhood infections. It was, in fact, considered desirable to catch the childhood illnesses, in order to acquire immunity early in life. The result was inevitably a series of epidemics at school: mumps during Trinity term 1944, with spectacularly swollen necks; German measles; and, by far the worst, whooping cough during Easter term 1942. The last produced a large dormitory full of sufferers with large white enamel buckets placed between the beds. As the epidemic died down a hard core were herded into a corner of the dormitory, each with his own bucket. As the most severe sufferers they produced spectacular coughs and fountains of vomit. Naturally, I was in this group. The only benefit of the mumps and whooping cough epidemics was the cancellation of term exams.

The only childhood infection acquired elsewhere was measles, which came out in 1938 when I was six and on home leave with my parents. We had gone to visit a friend, Mrs Palfrey, the widow of a chemist, in Alva, outside Stirling. My mother in her brisk way placed me in a darkened room. There I remained for two to three weeks. Their holiday in Scotland was spoilt and they were only able to go on the occasional expedition. One was to the Empire Exhibition in Glasgow. I still remember feeling hard treated because I could not go, even though my father brought back for me a lead model of the main tower.

These ailments were insignificant compared with some of the diseases then in Kenya. The most terrible was plague, endemic in the reserves, from which it was brought into the towns. My father had a brush with it. It was the practice for relatives of our Kikuyu servants to stay with them in the servants' quarters. A woman from a reserve came to us. The evening of the same day the houseboy came to my father, saying she was ill and needed to go to hospital. He did not indicate that it was urgent so my father said he would take her the next day. My mother and he went to bed. During the night the houseboy woke my father to say his relative was very ill. My father agreed to take her to hospital at once. When he went to the car he was surprised to find the woman and the houseboy already in the back of the car. At the hospital the houseboy let the woman fall forward; she was dead, and the hospital quickly established that she had died of plague.

My father returned home to take a bath in disinfectant. The servants were ordered to wash in disinfectant as well, their quarters were cleared and cleaned, and the car cleaned out. It was then just a matter of waiting to see what happened. Fortunately, no cases developed. I assume the relative had come from the reserve with the disease fully developed.

I was at school at the time of this episode. However, the plague epidemic was sufficiently serious for the boys at school to be given injections against plague. I wonder how effective they were. What was not in doubt was that they made us feel extremely unwell. The injection was given in the same way as all the others at school. We lined up and the same needle was used again and again, usually into the upper left arm. Towards the end of its life it became blunt and had to be pushed in hard. If this happened now there would be a shock-horror media campaign. We accepted this treatment and were perhaps more robust than today's carefully protected children. And the people administering the injections were not HIV-positive, nor were the other boys.

SPORT

I greatly enjoyed sport and it helped to make my time at Kenton more agreeable. The games fields were at the back of the hotel, and after a hot afternoon we would run up to the changing room to be first to have a drink of water from the metal urn with a tap. There were two metal mugs, which we used in turn, gulping down the tepid water. School reports had a section for sport and it gave me great pleasure to read for Christmas term 1944: 'Cricket 1st XI. Batting average 15.75, bowling 5.46. Has been a very useful member of the 1st XI.' The report the next term, my last at Kenton, stated: 'A very good hockey player indeed whose stickwork is at times quite brilliant.'

The master in charge of cricket was John 'Tik' Taylor. He was a stern coach in nets. Later I heard he was a homosexual, but he did not make a pass at me, even though I was invited to his room off the main (ex-lounge) dormitory in the evenings. Other boys received similar invitations to his room. Taylor was very keen to encourage success in the first eleven and when I was twelve he offered Shs 10/- (ten shillings) and a large bar of milk chocolate to the first boy to make fifty in a first eleven match. Both bribes were highly acceptable, for me the chocolate especially, as it was not available in term time and was in any case scarce during the war. My impression was that he wished another boy, one of his favourites, to win the prizes. In the event I did, by making fifty-six against the European Primary School in Nairobi. The same match was memorable thanks to a large Airedale grabbing a much smaller spaniel by the side. After desperate intervention by the spectators the Airedale released its victim, which ran off howling. I am sure my later success at cricket owed much to Taylor.

One cricketing event stands out in my memory: the visit to the school of members of the England eleven. They were out with the army and may I think have been an army eleven. In their whites they batted in the nets with the boys bowling at them. Wally Hammond, an England captain, was one of the group, and he was bowled by one of the school's opening bowlers, Grev Gunson, a member of a family with considerable sporting abilities.

The hockey first eleven captain was Ian Burnett, the son of the manager of the Standard Bank in Zanzibar, who stayed with us on his way to and from Zanzibar. Years later Ian and I were at Trinity, Oxford, together, and he became captain of the Oxford hockey team and a Scottish international. At Kenton Ian was centre forward and a prolific goal scorer.

At Kenton I also took part in athletics, for which, to my surprise, I received my school colours. Pole vault was my event. I also received my tennis colours, perhaps with more justification. All schools have a method by which boys may display their school colours. At Kenton, stars were sewn onto the band in school colours which went round the compulsory grey felt hat. Each sport had its position on the band.

The school was divided into three houses: Oryx (green), Bongos (yellow) and Kudus (red). We wore our house colours during house matches and results in the athletic sports went towards a house competition cup. However, we did not sleep in houses, and I do not think house loyalty was of much importance.

CRAZES

Like all boys we had crazes at school. They were part constructional – aeroplanes – part games and part collecting. The younger boys played hopscotch, using stones occasionally for throwing into the squares, but more usually lengths of key chain, which had the merit of not bouncing, rather like a golf approach shot with back spin.

Cigarette cards, which most brands included in their packets, were used for both games and collecting. The aim was to acquire as many as possible, especially of the rarer cards. The game consisted of flicking a card at ground level towards a wall from two to three yards. The boy whose card was nearest the wall won. The best position was to have a card leaning against the wall. The winner took cards from each contestant and threw them up. The cards which landed face upright were 'won'. We would play this game for hours.

Another game which must have been of Indian origin was what we called gillidunder (phonetic). This took place on the drive at the front of the hotel. A shallow and narrow trench was cut into the ground. A short piece of wood, cone-shaped at each end, was balanced across the trench. The player flicked the wood piece out of the trench with a stick. His opponent then tried to lob the piece back into the trench. If he succeeded, he won that round. If he failed, as was usual, the boy with the stick struck one end of the piece so that it sprang up into the air. He then tried to hit it as far as possible. If he missed he had another two goes. Three failures to connect ended his turn. The opponent then had a turn. If both had struck the piece, the one who had hit it further won the round. Again, this game went on for hours and was useful practice for ball games.

Being wartime it was inevitable that we collected the badges of all three services, of the Allies and of the Italians. Troops stationed in Kenya were asked to part with their badges, especially if they were in a newly arrived unit. I was lucky to be given by Bill Lane, a Railway colleague of my father who later became mayor of Tewkesbury, the cap badge of the Wiltshire Regiment which he had worn during the Great War. Another source was the Indian tailors on Government Road (now Moi Avenue), who occasionally had UK-made badges but mostly their own local badges, cast in low-grade metal. During the holidays of my last two years at Kenton I would wander from home down to the shopping area on badge hunts. There was never any worry about my safety. Back at school much swapping went on.

After the war I continued to collect. The best haul was from a tailor in Scotland, I think St Andrews, who handed over to Ian Burnett, with whom I was staying, and me boxes of badges of the Scottish regiments. My elder son, Adrian, now has the collection and is still collecting.

As was usual in Kenya, we were allowed to have 'pets' at school. These consisted of chameleons, the three-horned variety being most favoured. They would be kept in boxes and cages. The game was to guide them across foliage and materials, such as books, and watch them change colour to match their background. It was considered unfair to put them across anything red as it was thought to upset them – some boys even suggested that they might explode.

Some boys caught tarantulas by inducing them out of their holes in the ground and then used them for fighting. The tarantulas were kept in glass jars. If two were caught they would be put into a large jar to see if they would fight each other. They occasionally did, with the result of one being stung to death, an event regarded by the spectators as most satisfying.

Like most boys, we played Cowboys and Indians and other war games, in the bushes beside the long drive. In our informal cricket games we took on the names of famous cricketers such as Bradman and Hammond. One name we adopted was Stirling; quite why was not obvious.

Kenton was a fairly tough place and my first years were made miserable due to the teasing I endured. I must have been seen to be in some way vulnerable, perhaps a bit spoilt. I learnt to cope with teasing by ignoring it so that my tormentors ceased to be entertained. Boys (and girls) can be horrible to each other. One episode I remember without pleasure was being invited with a friend to the farm of a boy at Kenton. It was on the edge of the Rift Valley and raised above the valley. I remember the farm sounds in the early morning and the dazzling and continuous lightning displays at night along the hills in the valley. My friend and I ganged up on our boy host, why I cannot remember, and threw mud and stones at him. His parents had to intervene.

Towards the end of Kenton I realised with surprise that I was beginning to enjoy school. I was getting older and more senior; also, my success at games helped, as it has done through the rest of my life. The experience toughened me and taught me to value greatly the many moments of pleasure and happiness since then.

I must have learnt something at Kenton, certainly of the basics. At least it provided a base on which the masters at King's could build. I did learn one lesson in particular: that determination to succeed did produce results. In the lower forms I was usually top or second top. On one occasion my weekly position dropped to second after a run at the top. I was put out by this and resolved to get back to top. Next week I did.

HOLIDAYS

Holidays or local leaves were usually on the coast or trips into Uganda. The first, in 1937, involved the train to Kampala, bus to Butiaba, where my parents had friends in charge of the port, a steamer, the *Robert Coryndon*, to Pakwach and a paddle steamer to Nimule. The *Robert Coryndon* had the dubious distinction of having been constructed for the Great Lakes in Canada, with the result that the cabins near the engine room were oppressively hot. At Rhino Camp on the way to Nimule my parents went to look for white rhino, without success. The trip involved a visit to Murchison Falls (now Kabarega Falls), where the Nile passes through a narrow channel as it drops towards Lake Albert. A launch from the steamer took us to the falls.

On a second local leave to Uganda we climbed up to the falls again and then went ashore at the foot of the falls to feed an enormous and disgusting old crocodile. One of the crew skewered a large fish, probably a Nile perch, on the end of a long stick, which he held out to the crocodile. The offering was clearly expected and graciously received. I have a cine film of the event.

We were in Malindi at the outbreak of the Second World War, an event of which I have no memory. We had other holidays there, always staying at Lawford's Hotel. One holiday began badly, with a torch being stolen from the car as we crossed the Kilifi ferry. What I remember about these holidays is the exhilaration of surfing, on a wooden board, and being tossed about by the breakers. I also remember vividly the consequences of staying too long in the sun on the day we arrived in Malindi. The tops of my legs were so badly burnt that the skin cracked. So I spent a week in the shade having calamine lotion spread regularly on my legs. I did seem to be affected by the coastal sun and have disliked sunbathing ever since. During a Mombasa holiday once I got sunstroke and had to lie in a darkened room, having only soda water to drink.

Despite these problems and others – such as being stung on the head by a hornet which had its nest in a cave behind the beach below the Railway bungalow where we were staying, and cutting my feet on the sharp coral – the coast was a paradise. The pleasure began with the train journey, at a steady pace, from Nairobi. The train left at 5 p.m. so it was possible to watch the game on the plains before nightfall an hour or so later. Then a meal in the restaurant car, during which the bunks were made up in our compartment. I always chose an upper bunk. Lying in a comfortable bunk with the sound of the wheels over the rail joints was most soothing and I slept soundly, only waking when we stopped at stations such as Voi, which linked with the Tanganyika Railways. In the morning the countryside had changed. It was warmer, more tropical and more scented. There were various landmarks which increased my excitement: the place where the railway looped under itself in order to lose height, the first smell of the sea, the point when there was a first glimpse of the sea and finally the crossing of the bridge onto Mombasa Island.

Another memory of the holiday in Mombasa when I was stung by the hornet was waking on the first morning. I was still able then to sleep so soundly that the change of bedroom did not register at first. The realisation that I was on holiday and the sky was clear was special. But on this occasion it was made perfect by a bird singing on the bush outside the window; a song of total purity against a background of almost complete silence.

One holiday in Butiaba staying with friends, the Gordon-Cummings, stands out. I was ten. The Gordon-Cummings, in charge of the port there, had two beautiful daughters, on whom I looked with great approval even at that age. My father was taken shooting. We still have the trophies: hippo teeth and an elephant's foot. I also shot my first and only game bird, a guinea fowl, with a .22 rifle. It was perched at the top of a tall tree. I took ages over aiming, fired, and it dived away towards the ground. It was difficult to find even with dogs but eventually it was discovered looking like a stone.

The last home leave before the war was in 1938. We went down the Nile from Uganda, by ship to Marseilles, train to Paris and by plane to Croydon. The plane was a DH Albatros – an unfortunate name, I should have thought. Our plane was I think called *Frobisher*. As we approached Croydon I was riveted by the sight of vehicles moving on the road below. This leave coincided with the Munich crisis, and I remember being issued with a gas mask.

In London we stayed at an hotel in the Cromwell Road. It had a nursery into which the children were placed so the parents could go out unencumbered. A nursemaid took us to play in Kensington Gardens. I can remember running away and being generally disobedient. *Snow White* came out in 1938 and as a great treat my mother took me to see it. The sequence in which the witch is chased up the cliff was too much and I ran out of the cinema, refusing to return, to my mother's irritation.

The only long leave during the war was to South Africa in 1942. The flight started in Mombasa. We went in a flying boat, the *Canopus*, the first Empire flying boat to be built (in 1936). I thought it was Imperial Airways but it must, given the date, have been BOAC. I remember the water splashing on the wings as we took off and landed. As it was wartime the windows had to be covered by blinds as we took off. It struck me even then as absurd, because one could look at the warships in Kilindini Harbour with ease as we were taken by launch across to the plane moored in Port Retz. I was reminded of this absurdity during a visit to Ethiopia in 2000, while the war with Eritrea was still going on. Susan and I were flying to Lalibela to see the rock churches. On the way the plane landed at Bahir Dar, which is also an air force base. The blinds had to be drawn. The boarding and alighting passengers walked across the tarmac, where they could see the air force planes.

The *Canopus* stopped at Lindi, Biera and then at Lourenzo Marques for the first night. The second night was at Vereeniging, on Vaal Dam, in South Africa. We reached Durban on the third day. The journey was spoilt by excruciating toothache. I had to be doped to be able to sleep at all. In Durban the dentist removed the offending two teeth, whose roots had rotted.

During this leave we stayed in Ladysmith at the Crown Hotel, owned by Brigadier Otto Jones, whom my parents had met in Nairobi when he came with the South African troops. This visit was marked for me by the sight of shells, fired into Ladysmith during the siege, clamped to the pillars of the shop arcades, the remains of the trenches surrounding the town and the countryside with its aloe plants. We then moved on to visit my uncle Jack, who lived at Leopaardsvlei. Behind the hotel in which we were staying I saw a chicken being beheaded and then running round the yard, a horrifying and fascinating episode. The return journey to Kenya took us through Rhodesia, the Congo, where we went by train and on a steamer along the Lualaba, and finally through Tanganyika, by train. Such a journey was one of the benefits of empire. My school report for December 1942 records that I arrived late for the term.

Nairobi during the war was a marvellous place for a boy. There was no fear of being attacked if one wandered, so there was great freedom. The plains came up to the foot of the bluff above what was then the RAF station and is now Wilson Airport. So there was game in abundance close to Nairobi. Hyenas, with their whooping yell, could be heard at night. The sound still gives me a thrill and for me epitomises my time in Kenya. A visit to Lone Tree, where lions could be found, in what is now the Nairobi National Park, was quite an expedition. In early 1947 the area just beyond the airport became the Nairobi National Park so game can still be seen with ease. The improvements in the roads in the park have also shortened distances. A visit to Lone Tree is now a quick drive. What has changed is the development beyond Eastleigh. During the war trains going to Mombasa went onto the plains almost as soon as they left the station. When one was settled in one's compartment it was possible to see Thompson's gazelles, zebras, wildebeest and hartebeest.

Between 1935 and 1938 my father owned a motor cruiser on Lake Naivasha. We would drive there at the weekend and take it out on the lake. Part of the weekend ritual was cooking lunch on the boat over a Primus stove. My father always had difficulty starting the stove and would mutter and swear until the paraffin ignited under pressure. My memory is of sausages sizzling in the pan. Some time after the launch had been sold, my father and I climbed Longonot, an extinct volcano crater in the Rift Valley. We got up before dawn, drove towards Nakuru, parked the car and climbed in the very early morning, when the scents of Africa are at their sharpest. The climb took us a couple of hours and we were in good time to have a picnic on our return to the car. I was very close to my father on such occasions.

The gun laws appeared casual. Like most boys I had an air gun. It was a Daisy, which fired round pellets rather than the pointed lead pellets of superior air guns. Perhaps this was a deliberate choice by my parents. It was useless as a killer of even small birds. I once shot a long-tailed mousebird at point-blank range. The shock of the pellet dropped the bird, but by the time I reached it the bird was flying away. An army officer, a friend of my father, who was in the campaign against the Italians in Abyssinia (Ethiopia), brought back to Nairobi on leave an Italian carbine with a long bayonet attached to the end of the barrel by a hinge. He gave it to my father, who tried it on a range and discovered that it was wildly inaccurate. My father's proper rifle was an 8mm Mauser, a beautiful gun, though I do not remember him firing it much. I was presented with the carbine as a toy to use in war games. As far as I know there was no question of getting a licence.

For some time during the war I collected butterflies. My father took me to the Langata Forest, then well outside Nairobi, with a net and a jar for killing the butterflies. Trophies were taken home to be set on a special board with a narrow groove for the body. The wings were held in place by strips of paper pinned to the board. Sixty years after their capture I still have an airtight box of butterflies, some in fair condition, but others rather moth-eaten. Their names continue to give me pleasure: gaudy commodore, African monarch, noble swallowtail, orange dog citrus swallowtail, green-veined charaxes, narrow blue-banded papilio, gigtree blue.

Chapter 5

Transition (King's School, Canterbury)

In 1944 my parents decided that I should go to the UK for the rest of my schooling. They chose King's Canterbury, from a shortlist which included Campbell College in Belfast. The Common Entrance exam taken at Kenton was, I suspect, a disaster. Canon Shirley (Fred), the headmaster of King's, indicated as much to my father. He probably took me on the basis of meeting my father and the expectation that my father could afford the fees at a time when King's was about to return to Canterbury, and he wanted to increase the numbers at the school. Fred was a strong influence during my time at King's. He showed me great kindness in a number of ways: he sorted out a health problem by sending me to a specialist in Harley Street and encouraged me, when I was working for my scholarship exam to Oxford, by allowing me to read and browse in his library at home. One evening, when I was reading in his library, he brought in a glass of port and invited me to drink it. It was smooth and delicious. After my first sip he asked me how I liked it. When I replied with enthusiasm, he said: 'I should think so; it's Cockburn "03"!' Another link was his love of sport; he was a vociferous supporter of the school during rugger matches. His enthusiasm sometimes resulted in him getting onto the pitch during exciting moments. On one occasion, when I had the ball near the touchline, I shouted at him to get out of the way. It did not worry him.

In March 1945 my mother and I, together with Rita Thompson, who was due leave, went to the UK. As in 1938 we again went down the Nile route, which took about three weeks. We took the usual KUR&H train and steamer route as far as Nimule; from Nimule to Juba by car; steamer through the Sud from Juba via Malakal to Kosti; train to Khartoum, where we stayed for a few days; train from Khartoum through Atbara to Wadi Halfa; steamer to Shellal; and finally the overnight train from Shellal (Aswan) to Cairo, where we spent a week. Such a journey would be impossible now.

The long stretch between Juba and Khartoum was in a stern-paddle steamer. It was hot and humid, particularly in the Sud, which consisted of papyrus stretching further than the eye could see. The evening sun, a copper colour, reflected on the water as on metal. On top of the flat-roofed steamer, and well in front of the funnels at the stern, was a mosquito-netted 'room', used by the men. It caught the breeze created by the movement of the steamer and did something to reduce the oppressive heat at night. For a few nights I went to sleep in it, my poor mother staying in her stifling cabin. On board was the Sudan Railways official responsible for catering on the Nile steamers. He had, with my mother's support, taken me in hand, making me turn out neatly dressed and with brushed hair for the evening meals. Unfortunately, he was a homosexual, who took the camp bed next to mine in the 'room'. He held my hand and began to move his into my bed. I froze, terrified. Eventually he gave up and removed his hand. It was the only pass, such as it was, that has ever been made at me. I did not tell my mother but decided not to sleep up top again.

My only memory of Khartoum was the zoo, where a delightful young gazelle followed us about, hoping for, and getting, pieces of food. In Atbara, the headquarters of the Sudan Railways, we stayed briefly with Darvell, the Chief Accountant, my father's opposite number. In contrast to the desert, Atbara was marvellously green and lush, with irrigation channels running through the gardens of the club, where we were taken for a swim. With so much water it was incredibly humid. It was the only occasion in my life when I found it impossible to dry after a swim. As soon as the towel was removed I was damp with sweat. I gave up and dressed damp.

Between Wadi Halfa and Shallal the steamer stopped at Abu Simbel so we could see the rock temples, as we had done in 1938. The contrast between the glare of the sunlight by the river and the dark of the temples was so great that inside the temples seemed absolute black. The other point which struck me was that, from a distance, the statues did not look large. It was only close to that their enormous size could be appreciated. Near the Aswan Dam the steamer went past the Philae Temple, then still underwater – a sad sight. It was a pity we had to go by overnight train to Cairo. I remember being upset that it had not been possible to see Luxor. I had to wait until 1992 to do so. In Cairo we visited the usual tourist places: the pyramids, the fort, the Blue Temple and the museum where we saw the Tutankhamun exhibits. We also went to the bazaar where we had coffee in a shop and my mother bought a scarab on a gold pin, which Susan now has.

The final leg of our journey was by ship from Port Said to Gourock on the Clyde. The ship, the P&O SS *Chitral*, was a troopship taking 4,500 soldiers back to the UK. We went in a large convoy with Royal Navy destroyers and corvettes protecting us. There were no excitements, though our protectors did drop depth charges in the Irish Sea.

At the beginning of May my mother and I went by train to St Austell and then to the Carlyon Bay Hotel, where King's had settled for the war. Our arrival coincided with the end of the war in Europe. Consequently, the school was taking two days off. One of the entertainments was a school sing-song. There were wartime songs: *Roll out the Barrel, She's Coming round the Mountain*. We also sang traditional shanties, which made me realise how little I knew of them. I could not understand why the drunken sailor was put in a longboat called '*Tilly Sober*'.

For me, Cornwall in the summer term was a magical place. The sound of seabirds on the cliffs always recreates the memory of what seemed to be sun-filled days. Hydrangeas flowered in great clumps along the roads above the cliff. As a new boy I was both a school and house fag. The former involved me with other first-year boys in putting chairs away after concerts or lectures. The latter was more demanding, as the fags were on a dining room rota, which required them to set the tables. There was a shortage of cutlery, presumably because the school was not going to replace it shortly before our return to Canterbury. As fags were expected to find cutlery for their table, it was necessary to rise at around five in the morning to queue to collect it. Knives were particularly desirable and would not be left on the top of the long table in case they were pinched, but concealed by being stuck beneath the bar running along below the table. Getting up early did not worry me but washing up the school's mass of plates and cutlery after meals was disagreeable. When we got to Canterbury these duties ceased.

That summer we went on holiday to Mevagissey, staying in a boarding house just above the harbour, called the Cot. The holiday coincided with VJ Day and bonfires were burnt near the harbour.

The autumn term we returned, a little late, to Canterbury. My house, Meister Omers, was in a building at the east end of the cathedral. It was basically a twelfth-century house with floors inserted in the reigns of Elizabeth I and James I. The original fire place, some twenty feet wide, was in the senior boys' common room; it is now part of the house master's accommodation.

The winter of 1945 was my first in England. At the end of the autumn term, when we were allowed to decorate the house, holly was collected in the area of St Martin's. The glitter of the frost on the ground as we returned to school along the lanes and the crispness of the air were new and beautiful.

My father came to the UK on leave in 1946 and my parents returned to Kenya later in the year. I then stayed with my guardian, Roy Whitehorn, in Cambridge. In the summer holidays I went to Mrs Beith in either Sonning or Wargrave, where Rob Beith and I swam in the Thames or rowed on it or played tennis. Mrs Beith was kind and treated me like a son, preparing my trunk for the return to King's at the beginning of the autumn term.

Meister Omers

My father had bought a plot of eight acres in Limuru on which to build a house. The situation in Kenya just before the Mau Mau rebellion must have made him change his mind. The plot was sold. So why Alderney? In 1946 he had visited Alderney at the suggestion of Ronald Hoskins, who had been the Captain of one of the Railway ships and been posted to Butiaba. My father was also friendly with a senior official in the Home Office who had some responsibility for the Channel Islands and encouraged him to consider Alderney which had the additional advantage that his pension would go further. Moreover, he just liked the place. Our first home was in Chateau L'Etoc, a mid-nineteenth-century fort on a point at the lower end of the island. In winter storms the spray fell into the courtyard. Later we moved to Les Rocquettes, a house looking up Victoria Street. I had a room on the top floor overlooking the garden, which was full of gladioli.

Alderney, particularly out towards Chateau L'Etoc, had a strange atmosphere. I attributed this partly to the German slave labour camps,

My parents, 1945

whose occupants worked on constructing the island's fortifications, and partly to the use of the island as a burial place for the French mainland in Neolithic times. I enjoyed walking in the countryside at night. Alderney was always a bit unusual. During the Second World War the islanders were evacuated, except for one man who agreed to stay to look after the livestock and who, after the war, was ostracised by the returning islanders as a collaborator. The method of sorting out ownership of the belongings that survived the German occupation was, in my view, characteristically lawless. Any articles not claimed were put at one end of the Butes, a flat space that had been the archery butts. The islanders gathered at the other end and at a signal ran and seized any articles that took their fancy. Islanders who returned later could not claim back their property. This event was known as the 'Battle of the Butes'.

In July 1948 I flew to Nairobi. The journey took three days in an Avro York of BOAC. The first day we flew to Castel Benito in Libya, where we had dinner and spent the night. We were up early the next morning for the leg to Khartoum, where we spent the second night in a hotel beside the Nile. Up early again for the final flight, to Eastleigh Airport in Nairobi. It was a very civilised way of travelling.

By 1948 my parents had moved from No. 1 Ngong Road to a bungalow on the corner of Whitehouse Road and Rawson Road. Times had changed. There was expanded metal on the windows. Even so, thieves using long poles still managed to remove clothes and objects. They tried but failed at my parents' house. For me, it was a joy to see for a short time my beloved cat Twinkle, who sadly had to be left with friends when we went.

The return voyage from Mombasa was in the *Good Hope Castle*, a Union Castle cargo ship which took a number of passengers. Its main cargo was animals for the zoos of Europe. They included a camel, buck of different kinds, monkeys, warthogs, cheetahs, leopards and lions. Most of the leopards and cheetahs were young. The bulk were placed at the stern. This was highly desirable, for the monkeys' cages soon smelt strongly. There was no bar to going up to the cages, and I foolishly put my right hand too close to one occupied by a leopard cub, which hooked a finger with his claw. The only way to free myself was to pull. The result was a long neat cut, whose scar I still have. The ship's doctor put some plaster over the cut and that was that. The cheetahs were particularly attractive, both the grown animals and the cubs. The latter were allowed on deck on a lead. Sadly, the smallest died. The only other loss was a warthog, which somehow escaped from its cage and jumped overboard. In the Red Sea another boy and I would lean over the bow to catch the breeze and watch the dolphins swimming and leaping just ahead of the bow.

I now spent my holidays in Alderney. Although I once went by cargo boat from Weymouth, sleeping in a bunk normally used by the first officer, I usually flew from Gatwick, then a small airfield with a small circular terminal and no restrictions where one could wander. As flights were rarely on time I was able to walk along the runway to the abandoned grandstand of the Gatwick racecourse. The planes were a mixed lot, mostly Rapides, but once an ex-RAF Anson in which I was the only passenger. It had a circular window in the floor and, as the seats were uncomfortable, I was allowed to wander about the fuselage, hardly a cabin. There was also the pleasure for me that it flew low over the sea. Approaching Alderney's airport, planes appeared to be heading for the cliffs at the end of the grass runway. At the last moment they popped over the cliffs and landed.

I do not propose to write much about King's but just to highlight a few areas. The first was the music. I first became really interested in classical music when listening to BBC concerts on the portable radio given by my mother. I was then staying with my guardian, Roy Whitehorn, at 2 the Bounds, Westminster College, Cambridge. The piece of music that turned me on was Beethoven's 3rd Piano Concerto.

Canon Shirley believed that it was important for the school to hear performers of the first rank. The result was concerts by Frederick Thurston, Moura Lympany, Gerald Moore, Dennis Noble and others. Kathleen Ferrier came twice. These concerts took place in the chapter house because our assembly room was too small for the full school. It was possible to measure the effect of a talk or concert on the boys by the amount of shuffling and scraping of shoes. When Kathleen Ferrier sang, there was not a sound.

R. H. (Sam) Prior, the Meister Omers house master, was keen on music and would invite senior boys into his study to listen to records. He introduced me to Schubert's 'Trout' Quintet. Sitting on his sofa I became so absorbed in the variations movement that I felt a physical sensation of my mind turning over. We also listened to music in the school study I shared with Rob Beith and Basil Lee. The latter had a number of records – I remember in particular the *Force of Destiny* overture. Basil was a senior scholar who, after passing Higher Cert in Latin and Greek, took sciences in one year so that he could read medicine and become a doctor like his father. He went to Cambridge, where he also got a hockey blue.

One of the most memorable musical events was a visit to Vienna in 1949 with three other boys, organised by Tony Wright, the assistant music master. He later married Catherine Lacey, the actress, and told me that he had to leave King's when he became a Catholic. The trip began badly; we missed the train at Victoria because Tony had confused the time of departure. The journey took two days, as we had to take local trains and to spend a night in the mountains of Austria in order to catch the next local train. It was cold, April, and I had my first experience of sleeping under a duvet. Vienna was then still under joint Allied occupation, but it was the musical centre of Europe. We stayed in the British zone, in the Hotel Erzhog Reiner. We crammed in as much as we could but especially the operas at the Theatre an der Wein: the *Magic Flute*, *Werther*, *Der Rosenkavalier*. There were trips to the Vienna woods, the Kuntshistorisches Museum, where the Brueghels made a great impact on me, and the Belvedere Palace.

Tony Wright, who had known Vienna before the war, had an introduction to a lively and attractive Viennese girl called Jerry. She travelled with us to the UK on our return, when our diet consisted of hard-boiled eggs and rolls, with predictable results. She told us that she had been engaged to a dentist in Switzerland. We asked why she had ended it. She said the event which caused the final break was her birthday. Her fiancé gave what he obviously thought was a valuable and, from his viewpoint, prudent gift: free treatment for her teeth. She did not think a man of such little imagination was for her.

Sport played a large part in my life at King's. I played cricket for the first eleven for five years, rugger for three and hockey for three. The training at Kenton paid off. The cricket coaches were, again, remarkable. Alan Ratcliffe had made a double century for Cambridge before the war, but his record was overshadowed by a slightly higher score by the Nawab of Pataudi for Oxford in the same year. My other coach was Frank Woolley, of England. My last summer term, after I had won a minor scholarship in history to Trinity, Oxford, involved very little work. The only subject I took any interest in was, strangely, medieval Latin. So I was free to paint scenery for the school production of *Twelfth Night,* with incidental music by Anthony Hopkins, and play plenty of cricket. The result was 720 runs and four centuries. In *Wisden* for 1951 I was given the name of P. J. Wacker – appropriate, given my style of batting.

While at King's I had joined the Buccaneers Cricket Club, which had a close link to the school. It was founded in 1932 by Geoffrey

Moore, who lived until 2006. Richard Norris and I went on two of the club's Sussex tours, when we stayed at the Angel in Midhurst. I made plenty of runs and greatly enjoyed the relaxed friendship of the older members of the touring party. One match in, I think, 1948 was against Sir Anthony Titchbourne's eleven on his private ground at Titchbourne Park. It started at the usual time of 11.00 but there was a greatly extended lunch hour, helped by the crate of gin bottles in the lunch tent. The game after lunch was curious. One of the most drunken Buccaneers bowled brilliantly, helped perhaps by the state of the batsmen, and we won easily.

The cathedral overshadowed our lives at King's. It was a special environment, and its atmosphere has never completely left me. Immediately after the war there was scaffolding up the side of the cathedral. This enabled some of us to climb into the roof area of the cathedral and wander about above the quire and nave. The cathedral library was still in ruins and the area of the town near the Christ Church gateway had been flattened by bombing. There was remarkable freedom, especially at weekends, when we could wander about the Kent countryside. In summer there were cherries to buy (my only formal beating was for squirting cherry stones at the top table). We were allowed into town but not to cinemas, though, of course, we did go.

My last report from King's contained comments from my house master, Sam Prior, and from Canon Shirley. I record them out of pure vanity.

> R. H. Prior: He has been a great help this term in the house, often handling difficult circumstances with great tact and good sense, and I am most grateful to him. I do congratulate him on his many successes in every department of school life – not often does a boy achieve high academic distinction as well as success in all forms of sport – and I am also so very glad he has wide interests in music and art. He is a very talented young man and we shall miss him very much indeed. The very best of luck to him.

> Canon Shirley: He has played his part well through all the days of school life, and has helped to build it more firmly – by 'it' I mean

his school – and I am sure he will ever love it. If he contributes as much to Trinity, his college will be fortunate. But further afield I do believe he has a great contribution to make to society at large, which the heritage of Canterbury may help him to do. Not one here but wishes him a happy and good life.

OXFORD

In early 1951 I took the history scholarship examination for Trinity, Oxford. The exam took place in Keble hall so I have some affection for that college. I was certain that I had succeeded, not because the papers went well but as the result of a dream, in which I was batting in the Parks and playing a particular shot – which did happen later. Trinity gave me a minor scholarship worth £80 a year, a decent amount in 1951. I was told later that, if I had failed to gain a scholarship, I would have received a Ford studentship, also worth £80 a year, which was given to boys from King's going to Trinity. The intention had been that I should read law, and I was already in touch with the law don, Philip Landon, but it was suggested that I read history and I agreed. So I moved from Landon, whose company I would have enjoyed, to Michael McClagan, with whom I never established any relationship.

McClagan was a snob with a deep knowledge of the history of the noble families of Europe. During tutorials on European history it was easy to divert him by questions on the leading families of the period I took in European history (919 to 1274). Perhaps the problem was that I did insufficient work to produce decent essays for him on a regular basis. I was just not at ease with him as I was with other dons such as Robin Fletcher, an England hockey player. Our relationship did not recover even when I was getting senior in the security service. The morning after a Gaudy dinner we were standing near each other in the chapel quad. In a misguided attempt to compliment him I said he looked the same as I remembered. His reply was 'So do you'. He then turned away. So that was that.

My first two terms were preparation for history prelims. The set book was Bede's *Ecclesiastical History*, translated by McClagan. He must have done well from the sale of the recommended book. In the Hilary term I worked hard for three weeks and passed prelims. My work afterwards declined, except in those subjects which interested me: European medieval history and the French Revolution (my special subject). There were whole sections of English history, which ran from the Roman invasion to 1914, that I never covered. The late Middle Ages was one. When I had a viva, presumably to see if I could get a second, I had a fifty-fifty chance of getting one of the board's questions right. I could only guess. The answer was right; I rolled my eyes with relief, and the board laughed.

Without seeking an excuse for my idleness, it was a fact that the standard of lectures was generally poor; they were boring and badly delivered. I soon gave up most of them. Halliday, the Trinity dean, gave some worthwhile talks on the seventeenth century. On the other hand, I did enjoy lectures on other subjects which interested me, such as those by Lord David Cecil on Shakespeare's plays.

In our first year Richard Norris – also from King's and a brilliant hockey player, who was in the Great Britain Olympic side of 1956 – and I shared rooms in the Wren garden quad, which looked onto the gardens. We each had a bedroom off a large sitting room/study. Our scout, James, had worked for a Lady Jones before the war. He was a splendid person, helping us with our parties and knowing how to cope with us afterwards. He organised the staff at Susan's and my wedding reception. Susan's mother did not provide champagne but a very drinkable fizzy wine. James and his fellow scouts, serving the wine, wrapped the bottles in immaculate white napkins to disguise its true nature. James assured Mrs Hastings, in the confidential way he had, that no one would notice the difference.

There was no running water so our shaving water in the morning was brought up by James in an enamel jug when he came to wake us in time for breakfast in Hall. The loos and bath house, now demolished and built over, were towards the St Giles entrance to

Trinity and reached through a passage in the back corner of the quad. The deep and hot baths were one of the great pleasures of life after games. I threw myself into sport. On 18 October 1951 I had a freshman's rugger trial at Iffley Road and afterwards played briefly for Greyhound sides. At the same time I had a hockey trial and was soon playing for the university. I could not see myself being good enough to play rugger for Oxford; it was a time when the teams were dominated by South African Rhodes scholars. So I chose hockey, and in February 1952 played against Cambridge at Beckenham. We lost six–three. My contribution was two goals. Our goalkeeper, Ian Cory, was known as 'Angles' Cory because he had theories concerning the best way to defend the goal depending on the angle of the shot. In the event he failed completely to follow his theories; two of the goals were scored against him from very near the goal line!

In the vacation following that term, the Oxford side went on a tour of Holland which included the Amsterdam hockey festival, a highly enjoyable event. We were very fit so the late nights and entertainment made little impression. In The Hague we were entertained in a night club after the match. One of the Dutch team played marvellous jazz and we drank Dutch gin, Geneva. At the end of the evening, as we were climbing up into the street, I experienced a most extraordinary sensation, never repeated, that the top of my head was flat.

Trinity had a strong hockey team. In 1952 it had three blues, and in 1953 and 1954 five, three of whom became internationals. We won cuppers each year. Victory was followed by dinner given by the college; it came to be called the annual hockey dinner. These dinners were to the usual high standard of Trinity catering, which applied to all the meals. This was due to Philip Landon, who had been domestic bursar and was rumoured to have obtained food for the college on the black market during the war. We were not at all critical of him.

In the Trinity term of 1952 I had a freshman's cricket trial in the Parks, making seventy-seven. Colin Cowdrey made eighty-three. My cavalier approach to batting was not in tune with the rather dour style of the university side. The best I achieved was a 'B' fixture against

Oxfordshire, when I made some runs and took three wickets in one innings. One opportunity for fame was lost when Kent were playing the university. They were short of a player and wanted me to play for them. I could not be found. Most of my games were for the Authentics. I captained the Trinity eleven, not very successfully. I also played occasionally for the Buccaneers, the touring club I had joined while still at King's.

Financial reality caught up with me at the end of the first year. My father had arranged for me to open an account in Lloyds Bank in Carfax and made me an allowance of £620, which, with my scholarship money, should have been sufficient to pay the college battels and have something over for spending. I had not watched the level of spending and ended the year unable to pay all my battels. I had a long talk about money with my father, who was sad but not condemning. The result was that he would pay battels but reduce my allowance.

The second year Richard Norris and I moved to rooms above the old library opposite hall in the chapel quad. We each had our own

Scoring for Oxford, 1952

room, off the corridor leading to our shared sitting room, which looked one way onto the President's garden and the other onto the quad. They were some of the best rooms in the college. We held our first big party in them, giving about twenty guests Bronx cocktails, which were incredibly strong, and soon had them noisy and lively.

This was a year when I was very fit but also idle. The routine with friends from Trinity, especially John Strover and Lawrence Bryson, was to go after dinner in hall to the King's Arms at the end of the Broad and play bar billiards. There were also a number of agreeable parties in college, when champagne cocktails were offered. Some hosts offered Merrydown, a very strong, rough cider. After one such party at a house in St Giles, when I had mixed Merrydown with gin, I can remember setting out to return to college but have no recollection of walking across some busy streets and getting to my rooms. It was not a feat I have tried to repeat.

Life at Oxford was not just dances, parties and games, enjoyable though they were. My interest in music continued. There were concerts; a particularly memorable one was hearing Julian Bream playing in Balliol hall. It was my introduction to his guitar playing, and one piece sticks in my mind – Coros No. 1 by Villa Lobos. I also joined the University Opera Society, and in December 1951 attended the premiere in its Holywell rooms of Egon Wellesz's *Incognita*. I cannot pretend to have fully understood the piece, which has in any case disappeared from sight. Andrew Wilson, a fellow historian who had been head boy of Harrow, had rooms on the garden quad. He would invite friends to listen to records. Again, one set made a great impact: Schnabel playing Beethoven piano concertos, especially the slow movement of the 3rd.

The pattern set in the first two years continued into the third. I played hockey for Oxford in autumn and spring and Authentics and Trinity cricket in the summer. The main change was a move to digs outside college. Richard and I went for a term to a shared room run by a pair of spinsters in Wellington Square. We were too rackety for them and decided to move for the remaining two terms. We found rooms in a house in Kingston Road owned by Jan Janurek, a Pole, and his English wife Peggy (Smith). Jan had been in the Polish forces during the war, went to Campion Hall afterwards and was working in Thornton's bookshop. They already had two small girls. It was a friendly house, which we enjoyed enormously. It took me into a completely different world. The Janureks were devout Catholics so we met a number of Catholics at the university and outside. One was Susan Hastings, who visited while trying to reconcile two Anglo-Polish families, the Janureks and the Kocs, with whom she lived in Norham Gardens. We met in the kitchen and both later agreed that we were sure at the time that we were, in that hackneyed phrase, meant for each other. It did take a bit of time for us to sort our lives out as we both had boy-/girlfriends. Mine was Jenny Jowsey, a research scientist who later went to the Mayo Institute in the States; Susan's was a trainee accountant in Wenn Townsend, whom she had difficulty in shedding. I found juggling with two girlfriends, sometimes in the same house, rather a strain.

In my second year John Strover and I joined the Oxford University Air Squadron, which flew from the airfield at Kidlington. The squadron had Chipmunks as the basic plane but a number of the squadron graduated to Harvards (I did not). It was an amazing privilege to be able to fly free two or three times a week. After going solo we were allowed to take planes up and, though encouraged to practise certain manoeuvres, could do what we liked. It was exhilarating to perform aerobatics at a time when one did not have to worry about other planes. There were restrictions on low flying except with an instructor. I particularly enjoyed skipping over trees and fields. Another attraction of the air squadron was its mess in Manor Road. It was a comfortable place and had a large TV set, on which we watched the Coronation in 1953.

Each summer there was a camp. The first year it was at Middle Wallop; the next year, my last, at Ainsworth, on the Lancashire coast. One of the last operational Spitfires flew from the airfield out over the Atlantic to collect weather data. The weather was awful so everyone at the camp was given train warrants to go home. As there was no question of going to Alderney I went to Oxford, and it was during this visit that Susan and I got to know each other well. A dinner at the Elizabeth Restaurant in St Aldates was the highlight.

My time at Oxford was highly enjoyable. I should have worked harder but what I did reinforced my love of history. It also made me aware of England and the background to the life around us. The political parties seem to regard loyalty to England with suspicion. It is acceptable for the Scots and Welsh to have pride in their countries but the same emotion in the English (by which I mean the people living permanently in England) is 'right-wing', almost fascist. This is politically correct nonsense, because England is not a concept that can be suppressed. I was also able to indulge my love of games and music; and have two years' free flying. This may not seem much but it has been a solid background throughout my life.

Chapter 6

Starting a Career: Devonshire Course

In 1954 my father arranged through Bill (A.V.) Beith, the father of Rob Beith, for me to join the Union Insurance Society of Canton. I was interviewed and accepted – the first graduate to join the firm, which undertook marine insurance. The London Cornhill branch was headed by an experienced and much-respected underwriter. What I saw of him I liked. The programme for my future in the firm was three months in London and then a posting to Hong Kong for three years. My pay in London was £480 a year, and my father generously gave another £120. He had also supplied me with clothes for Hong Kong. They included two gabardine suits and a light dressing gown, which I still wear. My passage to Hong Kong was booked on the P&O *Oriana*. In Hong Kong I would be expected to mix socially and develop business contacts. Membership of the Hong Kong Cricket Club had been organised. Slightly older members of the firm on UK leave said that my salary after my first tour would be in the region of £3,000, an amazing amount to me and considerably higher than my father's pension (it did not rise before he died in 1962 – an example of the way the government treated its former employees).

In London I was mentored, in the way now fashionable, by a more senior employee who was fixed in London. Work seemed to consist of some reading about contracts but mainly in sticking clauses onto underwriting contracts. It was not intellectually demanding once one had learnt which clause had be stuck to which contract. It was reasonable to expect me to start at the bottom. There was no formal instruction; in Hong Kong I would learn on the job, under guidance. Nowadays this system is considered haphazard and unsatisfactory; we are expected to benefit from an endless stream of courses, a few of professional use but many, especially in the voluntary world of which I now have some experience, concerned with implanting political correctness. The perceived need for training, greatly encouraged by legislation, regulation and the result of court cases, has increased significantly the expenditure in organisations. People with experience who attend these courses are told what they have known for years, but in this wasteful way the organisation and individuals can demonstrate expertise.

One perk was luncheon vouchers. These were accumulated over the week, so that a group of us from the office could go to an oyster bar, where we would lunch on a dozen oysters, brown bread and porter – a drink I have never taken since. I still enjoy oysters.

My social life was full. I remember going to the Farnborough air show and being greatly impressed by the angle of climb of a flight of Meteors, which as soon as they had left the ground climbed almost vertically. This is now commonplace but was not so in 1954. I went to dances. One was in Nottingham, given by the parents of a girl I had met on Alderney. Her father was a Major General and her mother an ambitious Swedish lady. She was successful, in that her daughter married first the heir to a peerage and later another peer. She was a delightful girl and the dance was enormous fun. Whether I would have been acceptable to her parents is doubtful. I was fond of her, but I had already met Susan.

In September Susan went with her mother and sisters to Italy, where they were joined by her brother Adrian, then training to be a priest at Propaganda Fide College in Rome. She returned later in the month and I met her at Victoria station. Susan was determined to hide me from her family; anyone who knows the confidence of the Hastings family of being able to decide what is best for other members of the family (and everyone else) will understand her determination. Susan as the youngest of six knew just what this meant for her.

Susan decided to get a job in London. We saw much of each other, and by October 1954 agreed that we wished to get married. The implications for my job were considerable. We accepted that we would not be able to get married before I was due to sail, but would Susan be able to join me? If I left the firm, what would I do to support us? In the confident way of the young I was sure we could sort everything out. In fact I was probably too young to be married, but it worked and we are still together after more than fifty years. So I broke the news to the firm; they were horrified. It was explained to me that members of the firm were not allowed to marry until they were thirty. Before that age they were expected to devote themselves to their career. I said that such a wait was impossible, so they suggested a three-year tour after which we could get married. After discussion with Susan I rejected this also and said I would have to leave the firm. Later they offered eighteen months, but by then it was too late.

When my parents were told of the engagement my father flew over from Alderney and arranged for Susan and me to meet him in his club, the United Sports, which had its rooms in Whitehall Court and where my parents stayed when in London. He told Susan that she was ruining my career. It was difficult to have a discussion about such a matter in the club drawing room as it had to be conducted in whispers. When he realised that we were serious he did not continue the pressure. Susan was welcomed. Much later, when we already had two children, my mother, who was also in her own way very fond of Susan, told me that she would be on Susan's side when we divorced. She had read my horoscope, which predicted a divorce. My protestations that we had no intention of parting carried no weight.

I was sharing digs at no. 1 Kensington Park Road, Notting Hill, with David Rigby, who had joined Guthries. The house was owned by a homosexual who was an excellent landlord, though it was slightly disconcerting when he appeared at the front door with face powder put on in a hurry. During my father's visit to London, Susan was using our digs as a base. Early one morning we were in bed together (quite pure, as David and I shared a room!) when my father knocked on the door wanting to have breakfast with us. I hard-heartedly sent him away. I wonder if he really understood the reason for my apparent rudeness.

A brief period in general insurance in Susan's brother's firm in Maidenhead followed. He had agreed with C. P. Stevens, the head of the firm, that I should join on the same pay as in London. I lived in digs in Boyne Hill Avenue in Maidenhead but spent as much time as possible with Susan. I also continued to play hockey for Reading, and was given an England trial. I played for England B against Holland B in Amsterdam. I had been playing well, including in matches for the Hockey Association. Unfortunately, I did not play at all well in Amsterdam, and it was my one and only international game. In the summer it was cricket, usually for the Buccaneers.

When at school I had decided that I did not want to go abroad again. This resolution had been weakened by my acceptance of the Hong Kong job. Susan and I married in April 1955. It was soon clear to me and, I suspect to C. P. and Susan's brother, that I was unsuited to insurance. Apart from anything else, I am not a mathematician – and Susan's brother was a very good one. Moreover, I had not lived in England except when my parents were in Kenya, and was still interested in Africa. Those who have lived in Africa and come to love it know that one never loses the memory of the smells, the sounds and the feel of heat and space. At about this time the Colonial Service (which had become the Overseas Civil Service in October 1954) decided to reverse its preference for recruiting bachelors and take married men on the, correct, grounds that they were likely to be more steady. So I decided to apply to join the Overseas Civil Service as an administrative officer with a preference for Uganda. A more obvious choice, given my background, would have been Kenya, but I wished to go to a country without a settler problem where I could work with the local people.

DEVONSHIRE COURSE 1

I was invited to an interview on 22 August 1955 at the Colonial Office and beforehand sent details of a post which they would consider me for. I do not remember where but it was probably Uganda. On 1 September I attended a board, about which I remember little other than it was not too demanding. Perhaps my hockey Blue helped. On 16 September came an offer of a post in Uganda followed by a formal offer on 24 September. The whole process of recruitment was quick and painless.

My pay, which would be £816 a year, included inducement and a cost of living allowance. A £30 kit allowance was given in the UK and a further £20 when I arrived in Uganda. There was a warning that Susan would not be able to join me for six months. 'I am to explain that in view of the present acute housing shortage in Uganda it is not possible to permit wives and families to proceed to Uganda unless express permission has been granted by the Governor, and that this permission is not normally given during the first six months of an Officer's service.' In April 1956 I was told: 'The Governor of Uganda regrets that, as suitable housing will not be available, it will not be possible for your wife to accompany you at the outset.' In the event, a family house was allocated to us as soon as I arrived in Soroti, Eastern province. In fact, not a single wife was delayed. Gordon McKinnon's wife, whom he had married only a couple of weeks earlier, was the first to arrive, just in time to produce twins.

The offer was accompanied by masses of information on pensions, education, colonial regulations. Included was a marvellous booklet entitled *Preservation of Personal Health in Warm Climates*. The most horrific photo was of the sole of a foot covered with sores caused by jiggers (a flea that bores holes in skin, especially around nails, so it may lay its eggs). My life in Kenya had prepared me for jiggers, but for someone without experience of them the photo would have done the trick.

There were two overseas courses in Oxford: the first, 'A' Devonshire, for new entrants mainly for East Africa; and the second, 'B'

Devonshire, for officials with some experience. Overall we were a mixed bunch, from most parts of the Commonwealth. There were eight of us in the Uganda group. By chance, one, Gordon McKinnon, was a Canadian. The others consisted of two Ugandans, John Kaboha and Frank Kalimuzo (John was a princeling from Toro and Frank came from Kigezi); three married, Jim Barber, Gerard Barnes and myself; and two bachelors, Bill Clarence and Chris Olding. Only three of us are still living. Frank disappeared in the violence in Uganda when Vice Chancellor of Makerere University; Gordon McKinnon returned to Canada and died young; John Kaboha died of heart failure in Nairobi while waiting to return to Uganda after a career in the Commonwealth Secretariat, well away from Obote and Amin; Chris Olding died of cancer; and Gerard Barnes died more recently.

The most cheerful on the courses were the West Indians on the 'B' Devonshire. One was a former Test bowler, who was hit all over the ground by a pair of South Africans playing for the Cambridge courses in our annual match. Another had the delightful name of Wellington Friday. Some names stick for ever, like a man from Lango district in Uganda called Benjamin Benefit Kindly Odur.

Susan and I were already living in the basement flat of her mother's house on Iffley Road. I rejoined Trinity and was within easy distance of the Parks area, where most of the course was held. In February 1956 Susan had had our first son, Adrian, which put up our monthly allowance of £48 by £2 10s. The course supervisor was H. W. P. Murray and we were expected to join the Overseas Services Club for the sum of £3 10s 0d. for the period of the course. The course consisted of seven subjects:

colonial history;
colonial government;
law;
language;
anthropology;
land use in the tropics;
economics.

There were exams in the subjects, and failure 'renders the cadet liable to the cancellation of his selection'. On the assumption that the board selected the right candidates, which I think they did for the most part, I suspect one had to fail abysmally to be rejected.

The immediate impression of the course was that it was bitty, but in retrospect I think it gave a good basis to understand the situation in which we would find ourselves. I particularly enjoyed the anthropology, colonial history and colonial government. The last two, setting out recent events and developments such as Mau Mau and the expulsion of the Kabaka from Uganda in 1953, were of obvious relevance. As a group we were under no illusions that we would have a career for life. The process that would lead to the end of empire was obviously under way but we just accepted the situation.

The least successful part of the course was a visit to a county council – Buckinghamshire, I think. It added nothing to our understanding of government. The most valuable, at least potentially, was the course in Luganda given by Ron Snoxall and Earnest Sempebwa. We all passed Lower Luganda but it was obvious that a posting to Buganda and plenty of practice would be needed if we were to become at all proficient. My posting turned out to be to Teso, a Nilo-Hamitic area, with a language, Ateso, that was utterly different in its basic construction. In fact, my upcountry Swahili, acquired in Kenya, was of more use than Luganda, because many chiefs, especially the older ones, spoke Swahili.

In June a letter came from the Colonial Office, stating that they had received a satisfactory report on my performance during the course, confirming my appointment and telling me that I would be travelling to Mombasa on the *Dunnottar Castle* leaving on 25 July. The Crown Agents would pay me the £30 outfit allowance and I would receive half pay during the period of the voyage. I had been told that we were in theory entitled to first-class passages but we went tourist class.

After the course our time was spent in preparing for the move. Walters of the Turl supplied the safari equipment: two Hounsfield beds (£7 16s 0d.), canvas bath and basin with frame (£3 12s 9d.), which turned out to be practical and were used throughout our time in Uganda. We were strongly advised to get safari uniforms in Uganda. We had to pack trunks and arrange with my parents for the shipping of my mother's piano, a tropicalised Chappell baby grand which she had taken from Malaya to Kenya. There was the vexed problem of Susan's clothes. We were very low on money, though Susan's mother had been generous in her help. The advice of the wife of a senior official from Uganda, who had taken Susan to tea in the Cadena Café in Cornmarket, that she would need at least twenty dresses and 'a little fur stole for the evenings', had not been helpful. In the end she took eight dresses; Horrocks were a godsend.

VOYAGE TO MOMBASA

The *Dunnottar Castle* left from East India Dock. Susan, along with Adrian, my parents and Rob Beith, had received permission to come on board to see me off. It had been arranged through Mrs Beith's uncle Eddie, a Thames pilot. This infuriated Dame Vera Laughton Matthews, the wartime head of the Women's Royal Naval Service (WRNS), because her son, David Matthews, was going to Tanganyika but she had not been allowed to come on board. Farewells at the beginning of a voyage are a curious affair. One stands around finding things to say and appearing calm when the departing passenger is beginning to think about the voyage and everyone is wondering when to say the final farewells. An announcement made the decision for them to leave. They waited briefly on the dockside. As we began to move, Dame Vera, who had been shouting remarks up to David, strode along the dock with her hands in her side pockets, nautical fashion, occasionally removing them to wave energetically to David. It took half an hour to leave the dock. We then began to settle in. The baggage was piled up in a central gangway and we had to rummage for our cases needed for the voyage. The cabin, which I shared with three other cadets, was about the best of the tourist class and quite cool with its outside porthole. The steward was prepared to bring us tea in the morning.

In a letter to Susan I described the food as 'not bad at all'. The steward who served our table looked like an ex-boxer and his speed of service suggested that he was punch-drunk. He claimed to be having a holiday after spending two months in a South African jail for beating up a policeman. A missionary lady told him he would not go to heaven, to which he replied that he was happy enough here. The cadets took to him. I cannot remember feeling seasick, even when a brief but violent storm in the Red Sea cleared most of the dining room. The storm ended immediately after lunch! The only occasion when I was ill was in 1945, in a troop ship, the SS *Chitral*, going from Port Said to Scotland. The Mediterranean was very rough on our first

My parents with Susan, Adrian and Rob Beith

day out and I was ill after breakfast. I had to rush up on deck to be sick – over the correct side, I am glad to say. I returned immediately for another breakfast and had no further problems.

The cadets formed themselves into groups. Ours consisted of the Uganda cadets and David Matthews, Mure Smith and Wyn Riley going to Tanganyika. For much of the three weeks we played chatty bridge or liar dice. Otherwise we took part in the inevitable deck games competitions. There were dances, some fancy dress, or games such as 'horse racing' when model horses were drawn along a board (track) by string attached to rollers wound by enthusiastic passengers. I read a good deal or leant on the rail watching the sea, which had its own power to mesmerise.

The tourist-class swimming pool was canvas slung in a wooden frame. At the start of the voyage the water was covered in smuts from the funnel. It was cleaned later, when some of the first-class passengers started to use it. We were not allowed to use the first-class pool, but did so. We also enjoyed irritating the first class by wandering through their area of the ship.

The ship stopped first at Gibraltar, where David Matthews, a Catholic, and I went to Mass in a church in English Gothic style and then up the Rock in a taxi. The next port was Marseilles. There was the inevitable visit to Notre Dame de la Garde, a trip enlivened by one of our group having his pocket picked on the way down in the funicular. He lost £80 in travellers cheques. After a search we went to the British Consulate, to discover that the thief had posted the wallet, without the cheques, through the consulate's letterbox. Next Genoa. It was my first visit to Italy, and the old city was a revelation. Malcolm Norris, another Tanganyika cadet, and I wandered about the streets visiting churches and looking at the town houses with their courtyards and first-floor gardens. Malcolm was an ideal companion for this. He was an expert on medieval churches, especially their brasses, and was publishing a book on German, including East German, brasses. Susan and I needed carpets so I bought one for L400 (£2 10s.); it was not a good buy.

At Port Said we were able to take cameras ashore despite the growing crisis over the canal. This was more than I had been able to do in 1948 when visiting in the 'zoo' ship. I did not detect any particularly anti-British feeling, but as I said in a letter to Susan, 'the people are very pro-Nasser whom they consider to have done much for them. If it came to war (which I pray it won't) they will fight hard for him.' I bought another carpet and some sandals for £7, leaving £1 of the carpet money. It was a slightly better carpet but did not survive the first tour.

The Red Sea reached the usual high temperatures. In a letter I recorded, 'The night before last the temperature in the cabin went up to 125F, though I did not sleep at all badly. The water was 90F yesterday.' Many passengers slept on deck.

We reached Mombasa on 16 August.

> The shambles here is appalling – it has taken all day to collect our baggage, let alone see it through customs. Everyone shouts at each other and as soon as anything happens, the ship has to be moved along the berths. We have made two moves today.

Like most of the cadets I was out of cash, and we were allowed a small advance on our salaries. I bought white knee stockings to go with the white ex-navy shorts my parents had provided. This was suitable wear on the coast but not for Uganda, and I never wore them again. Another poor buy! A letter awaited me from Owen Griffith, the District Commissioner of Teso, who had visited the course in Oxford. We had been allocated an old house described by Griffith as 'not bad by local standards'. I did not know how to interpret that comment. The cadets going to Tanganyika were having a terrible time. Not one could go direct to his post; there were no convenient steamers, and the secretariat had given them all different postings to the original ones. David Matthews had a journey of some 900 miles, which was expected to take four days by road.

The train journey from Mombasa to Nairobi and, after a change of trains, to Tororo was a marvellous return to Africa, with its evocative smells and heat. After Nairobi there was the climb into the cool of the highlands, the dramatic descent into the Rift Valley and another climb to Timboroa summit, at 9,136 ft. Anyone who loves Africa never forgets its particular atmosphere. In 1995 I went as International Chairman of Leonard Cheshire to Botswana. It was the first return to sub-Saharan Africa after over thirty years. It produced the same effect. Going to the Cheshire Home along dusty warm streets, with people strolling along the edge of the road, brought back East Africa to me.

The train arrived at Tororo at 3.30 a.m. It took an hour to unload. Luckily, Bill Clarence, who was going to Northern province, had been sent a Land-Rover and was able to drop me in Soroti on the way. I am not sure how I was supposed to get to Soroti without Bill's help. Perhaps Owen knew about the Land-Rover, or just expected me to ring for a car to collect me.

Chapter 7

Teso District

I arrived in Soroti on 19 August 1956. Owen and Rosemary Griffith put me up and helped me through the problems of settling in. On 21 August I reported my arrival on duty to the Chief Secretary and Minister of Local Government in the formal style of communication with superior officials: UFS (which I was told meant 'under flying seal') the Provincial Commissioner and District Commissioner, who both had to endorse the letter. A few days later the PC swore me in. The good news was that we had received a pay rise and I was now on £939 p.a. The first requirement was to obtain a loan to buy a car, an Opel Caravan, which I thought would combine comfort with enough space to carry equipment on safari. The application went in on 21 August, together with a request for a set of the Uganda laws, and for the £20 outfit allowance. Then there were photos for a driving licence, the luggage to collect (more was coming from the coast), shorts and bush jackets to be ordered, and servants, a cook and houseboy, to be found with the help of Owen Griffith. On top of all this I had no money until my salary was paid. Thankfully, shopping in the dukas (shops) in Soroti was for the most part on credit.

On 23 August our house became vacant. It was an old bungalow with a large garden – no flowers but plenty of shrubs and trees, including mangos and guavas. It had been condemned, and during our time work was needed to replace the wood eaten by termites. In our view it was infinitely preferable to the modern government houses, and it must have been well built, as it was still up, with a garage added, and occupied when Susan and I visited Soroti in 1996 and 2000. The verandahs and windows were covered with mosquito netting so it was not necessary to sleep under a mosquito net, a boon in the hot weather. One of the evening tasks for the houseboy was to 'Flit' the house with a small pump-gun to kill any lurking mosquitoes. Whether it had any effect is doubtful. The floors were polished concrete and the houseboy polished them regularly. We were provided with basic furniture – beds, chairs and tables, as well as a filter and meat-safe for the kitchen. We took some furniture out ourselves, including the piano and a display cabinet, and bought cushions for the settee.

There was no electricity, though it was moving closer. We used pressure lamps, which produced a powerful white light, or, occasionally and mostly on safari, hurricane lamps. More articles to be bought. There was water supplied from boreholes with a faint brown tinge

Soroti house, 1957

Soroti house, 1996

from the earth. Later, water was pumped from a lake linked to Lake Kioga through a pumping station near the Awoja ferry, a crossing point on the shorter route to Mbale. The evening bath ritual began with a wood fire lit under a 44-gallon drum outside the house, from which a pipe led through the wall to the bathroom. The children, Adrian and later Nicholas, had the first bath; ours came later, after games or a walk. The loo was on its own at the end of the corridor past our bedroom. It had been placed almost separately to protect the rest of the house from its smells and so that the night soil porters (responsible for removing human excrement) could reach it without coming into the house. Mercifully, it had been converted to a water system before we arrived. The night soil porters still operated in the town; more about them later.

I have always had a fear of snakes. This was reinforced when a puff adder appeared at our back door and a young cobra at the front door steps. The servants killed the former and I, with a golf club, the latter. I also remember our returning one evening in the car from Serere and running over a thick blackish/grey snake which stretched across the road. It was like driving over a small 'sleeping policeman'.

Soroti consisted of two areas: the part occupied by the boma, (the Protectorate and Teso District Council offices and the Court House), and the government houses; and the town, with its mainly Indian-owned houses and shops. In the former the boma was in the middle of a road system laid out as a Union Jack, or perhaps a Scottish saltire. Our house was on the outer edge of one of the 'flag' verticals, not far from the European Club, which lay inside the 'flag'.

Our nearest neighbour was the magistrate, Hatch Barnwell, a bachelor who had served in the Indian Civil Service before Indian independence. He had the distinction of possessing a horse, which, unfortunately, died before our arrival of a condition picked up in Soroti. It did allow Soroti to be described as a one-horse town. He was succeeded by a newly married magistrate, whom we liked. His wife, totally unaware of the way of life in Africa, had the unusual practice of locking the servants in the house to make sure they worked. For shopping in the dukas, she wore hat and gloves.

The outstanding feature of Soroti was the Rock, which rose like a boulder for about 300 feet. It was said to be the home of a leopard, but I never saw any sign of it. The town lay on a plain out of which a number of other similar rocky outcrops rose. To the south of the district there was a gently undulating landscape with patches of swamp; to the north, which was much drier, the country was typical flat African savannah. There was plenty of rain but only in two seasons: the long and short rains. Before, over and after Christmas was the dry season. Towards the end of the dry season the heat and dust became increasingly trying, and sleeping was a sticky affair. The verandah outside my office in the old-style Protectorate offices reached 94°F in the afternoon. Normally our dress in the office was khaki shorts with long khaki stockings (or, less normally, long trousers) with a shirt and tie. There was no air-conditioning and, until electricity arrived, no fans. Even after electricity there were not enough fans for the offices of the junior ADCs. So, as a concession to the heat in the worst of the dry season, we were allowed by the DC to omit the tie. Towards the end of the season we would watch the sky for the build-up of cloud, the harbinger of the rains. It was a blessed moment when they broke. The clouds would form a dark line to the north of Soroti. At the beginning of the long rains, the rain would arrive in the middle of the day. As the season progressed it arrived later and later in the afternoon and became less heavy.

Soroti was not a particularly healthy station, and our children in particular suffered. In the past it had had a bad reputation for malaria and blackwater fever. The European cemetery under the Rock had the graves of a number who had died of blackwater in pre-prophylactic days, when medical services upcountry were sparse. We took Paludrine – a tablet a day – and, after a case of malaria occurred on the station, doubled the dose. There was a regular programme of spraying the streams and water around Soroti to kill the mosquitoes and their larvae. Towards the end of our tour Susan lost so much weight that she was only seven and a half stone. I had regular bouts of food poisoning, three in three months at one stage. Our health during our second tour in Ankole was generally much better.

Susan and Adrian arrived in Entebbe on 1 September. They had flown first class because Adrian was under a year old, a luxury which

Soroti from the Rock

made the journey easier. As the plane was late, having been delayed in Khartoum, and Adrian was tired, we stayed the night in Entebbe with the Marshalls. Don was an Australian, and Permanent Secretary in the Ministry of Local Government. He and his wife were most welcoming to a very junior administrative officer and his family. As our car loan had not come through, we had a government car to take us to Soroti. It kept stopping and having to be pushed to start again. There was always someone to help. It was one of the pleasures of Uganda that local people were always willing to help by pushing or lifting. It took seven hours to get to Soroti, and because it was a Sunday everywhere was closed. Our lunch was at a garage in Tororo.

Susan, without a word of Swahili, let alone Ateso, found the first weeks in the house difficult having to deal with the servants. She was also apprehensive of the sounds of Africa at night. Hyenas howled from near the Rock and even frogs made the unsettling sound of deep breathing.

SERVANTS

It was expected that we would have servants. This was particularly so in upcountry stations, especially the very hot, such as Soroti. They were essential on safari and their employment was an element in the local economy. In addition, some wives, including Susan, worked, so we needed an ayah to look after Adrian. When we arrived, cooking was done on a wood-burning Dover stove in a room next to the servants' quarters. When electricity came, Susan did the housework for a time, but her secretarial work increased to the point where we had to have a houseboy again.

Owen Griffith had selected two servants from the group available for employment: Odeke, a cook, and Juma, a houseboy. Odeke was an obvious rogue and an indifferent cook. He lasted only a few months. The final straw came when he was told to provide mutton stew for lunch and produced instead a solid lump of grey boiled meat. This event occurred when Salatieri Eyudu turned up at the boma asking if there was a post available. He was a clan chief from a village about six miles from Soroti, and had not been working because his wife did not like him sleeping away from home. I mentioned Salatieri to Susan, who immediately identified him as the cook described by other wives as marvellous but unattainable. We saw Salatieri and agreed that he could sleep at home. In fact, we enjoyed having the house to ourselves for much of the evening. Salatieri would cook supper, served by the houseboy, and they would then leave us. Later in the tour, when we had electricity, he would often leave our supper ready with the table laid. So we were agreeably alone. Salatieri was an outstanding cook, who produced varied and delicious dishes. One especially good dish involved light vol-au-vents, learnt in one session from Susan's mother. It was a bonus for our guests not knowing what they would have for dinner. On the other hand, we knew exactly what we would be given when we went to other houses: peanut soup, pork fillet or fish from Lake Kioga, and baked custard (known as custardi bake).

Salatieri lived up to his reputation. He had a real understanding of cooking and enjoyed looking through the *Good Housekeeping* cookery books Susan had been given as wedding presents. The trouble was that his suggestions for new dishes fell at the hurdle of our lack of money. In addition to his skill as a cook he was utterly honest, producing meticulous accounts of his purchases. A remarkable example of his conscientiousness occurred during the farewell visit of the governor, Sir Andrew Cohen. A reception was to take place in the DC's house for which the Administration wives were expected to produce 'nibbles'. News reached us that Salatieri's father had died. We wondered if it was his real father instead of a close relation. Was he avoiding the fiddly job of helping to make the 'toasties'? During the afternoon he turned up, looking terrible. It had been his real father, but he still made all the 'toasties' before leaving. As he had only been with us just over a month, this loyalty was outstanding. Because he had these special qualities, we paid Salatieri well above the going rate for cooks (in addition to the usual allowance of 1lb of sugar a week). We were not popular but it was just. Later in the tour I lent Salatieri money to enable him to put a corrugated iron roof on his house and deducted an amount each month from his pay.

Salatieri invited us to his house in the village where he was clan chief and introduced us to his wife, Lucy. All, as we expected, was neat and tidy. Later we took the body of a member of the village from Soroti Hospital to the village. The Opel was convenient for such a task, and there were other occasions when we took bodies to their homes. The reason was simple. If the relatives had to use lorries, the drivers charged extra for a dead body. Sometimes relatives would remove a person from hospital when near death to save money. The bizarre situation could occur when part of the journey, when the person was alive, would be charged at one rate and part at a higher rate if they died on the journey. One could also see bodies being transported on the back of bicycles.

Juma stayed a little longer than Odeke but he began to complain, unreasonably, about the amount of work he had to do. He also did not like going on safari, for which servants were paid an extra allowance. Eventually he went and we asked Salatieri to find someone whom he could recommend as a houseboy. He found Wilson, who stayed with us for over a year. Then, after a gap without a houseboy, we again turned to Salatieri, and he found William from his own village.

We also employed, briefly, two kitchen 'totos' – that is, general assistants. We did so mainly out of pity, as they were desperate for money. One was a Karamojong lad but the Iteso ganged up on him and, for the peace of the household, he had to go. The other, Dyemps, was a sad young man who looked like a teenager. He came from Ngora in the south of the district and was not respected by the other servants. When I was due to tour Ngora county, he asked to be given leave and a lift down there. This caused some amusement among the others. He went in the Land-Rover with the interpreter, whom I asked to find out why he was so keen to go to Ngora. It emerged that he was married to an unfaithful wife and he wanted to sort out the marriage. He never returned.

Ludya with Adrian

The final member of the household, who remained with us on and off throughout the tour, was Ludya, our ayah. Susan was reluctant to have an ayah as she had heard they were all prostitutes. Owen told her it was true for the most part but he knew of no case when children were mistreated. There was also the difficulty that, without an ayah, Adrian could not attend the morning and evening gatherings of ayahs and children, when the children played together. These took place under the trees beside a road leading up to the boma. So Susan agreed, with some reservations, to take one on.

Ludya was always neatly dressed and was highly efficient. She was in no doubt that she bathed Adrian better than Susan. However, she had her problems. She was desperate to have a child and her failure to conceive made her discontented. Suddenly, after eighteen months, Susan noticed she was washing all her clothes and wondered if something was going to happen. At the end of Adrian's second birthday party, at the end of February, she gave twenty-four hours' notice and left the next day. She said she was going to Kampala for medical treatment. Susan was so angry she tried to manage without an ayah but Nick was only six weeks old and Adrian missed riding his tricycle to the gatherings of the children and ayahs. Not wanting so strong a character as Ludya, we took on Lucy, a rather sad, slightly older woman. She had been employed by Asians and had not worked for Europeans before. She was adequate, but Adrian had grown fond of Ludya and missed her. In less than a year Ludya returned to Soroti and wanted her job back. She enlisted the support of Rosemary Griffith. Susan resisted, as she did not really like Ludya, but Adrian was becoming upset at the gatherings because Ludya joined them. So, reluctantly, we took Ludya back, but on condition she could be dismissed without notice if there was any further trouble. She stayed until Susan and the children went on leave to the UK and, as we discovered later, left with quite a few small knick-knacks which had caught her eye. She was keen on clothes, had an immense wardrobe and, when asked what she would like for a Christmas present, would always say (yet another) 'Dress'. She did dress well.

Her routine was to come in at 7.00 a.m. when the houseboy brought our early morning tea. If Adrian was not already up she would dress him and take him in the cool of the morning for a walk along the nearby roads. She would clean and sort his room, and wash and iron his clothes. Around 10.30 a.m. or 11.00 a.m. there was the morning ayahs'/children's meeting. Then lunch, followed by the afternoon rest. Ludya returned at 4.00 p.m. and took Adrian for the afternoon ayahs'/children's meeting. Finally, he had his bath and bedtime with Susan and me.

We, like most people, allowed our staff time off on Christmas Day in the evening. Some liked to entertain on Christmas Day. This did not always work well. We were told that a senior department official and his wife had tried to give a dinner party. They were in a hard drinking group, and returned home for dinner late after a long session in the club. They sat for the first course, soup. The servants carefully ladled the soup into the bowls. It was baked custard ('custardi bake'). The second course was demanded. Again, custardi bake. Same with the dessert. It was obvious that the servants were very drunk; but the message got through!

My first safari, lasting four days, began on 10 September, under the guidance of the DC. Susan and Adrian came with us. We had collected our car from Mbale a few days earlier. It too had stopped without warning on the way to Soroti and had been pushed by the usual, obliging, local people. My knowledge of cars was, and still is, limited, but by fiddling with the carburettor I persuaded it to go.

Our first stop was at etem (sub-county) Ongino in Kumi ebuku (county). Our camp equipment went in the office Land Rover together with the staff driver, our cook (Odeke) and the DC's servant. We took Ludya with us. When we arrived at Ongino there was no sign of the Land-Rover or of the DC. After an hour they arrived. The Land-Rover had, inevitably, broken down, in Soroti, so Owen had gone home for tea before setting out. We learnt two lessons: vehicles in Africa break down frequently, and never get ahead of the safari truck.

The rest camp was fairly typical of the sub-county variety (county rest houses were mostly permanent buildings with corrugated iron roofs). This was a series of thatched huts with mud walls. Usually the only furniture was a table, but sometimes a chair or two were provided. There was a hut for us (Owen slept in a tent on this occasion), another for the servants, a kitchen and yet another for the loo. The last consisted of a hole in the floor over a pit. One became accustomed to its use but I always had a slight fear that bees or hornets would emerge from the hole and sting me.

In Ongino the main hut had no doors and walls which only rose to waist height. It was divided by a grass partition between the sleeping area and, towards the entrance, the dining area. The floors were of beaten cow dung. This sounds awful but, in fact, it provided a clean floor and gave off, if newly laid, a pleasant fresh smell. The absence of a door worried Susan, who has a great fear of snakes. She tried to barricade the door gap with bits of our equipment which would not have prevented snakes getting in. Snakes generally preferred the thatch. She soon became accustomed to the style of rest houses we used. On this occasion we were vulnerable to the weather. Susan, in a letter to her mother, wrote: 'There was a terrible storm which swept right through the house, first of all a terrible wind that blew dust into everything and then torrential rain which poured through [the roof] but being English we found one dry spot and continued eating our tea.' We stayed two nights in Ongino.

SOROTI TOWNSHIP

There was no township officer, as there was in Mbarara, to oversee the running of the township. So it fell to the most junior ADC to do so. I took over from Edward Cunningham. The DC chaired the council but the day-to-day supervision fell to the ADC. As I have already mentioned, Soroti Rock dominated the town. On one side were mainly the shops and homes of the Asian residents, with a Somali 'squat' on the edge. This area was the subject of dispute and eventually I had to arrange their removal. On the other side of the Rock was the township store and the European cemetery. Beyond the store were night soil pits, called Otway pits, whose construction was completed in my time in Soroti.

The township labour force of around 250 were under a headman, Stephen Ejinat. Their duties included cutting the grass and clearing the anti-malarial drains, both necessary for health because these activities helped to keep down the mosquito numbers. Cutting the grass was also convenient for social reasons, in that it enabled the fairways of the nine-hole golf course to be maintained at government expense. The labour also swept the streets and removed the night soil from houses without septic tanks. The night soil gang of around thirty were special. They were great characters and, not surprising, considering their job, mostly half-drunk. They had a night soil cart, a closed tank, which just before my time was drawn by bullocks. It now had a tractor, which was slightly less temperamental than the bullocks. There was also a new cart. At the end of September I was introduced to the reality of the night soil gang. One night we had gone to bed fairly early as Susan was tired after several bad nights, probably with Adrian. Suddenly we heard men sounding merry outside, so I opened the window, to find the driver of the tractor which drew the night soil cart. He said he had lost his tractor and the night soil could not be collected. I dressed and went out to look for it. The obvious cause was the day driver taking it for a spree. I tried tracing him through his girlfriend, the doctor's ayah, but without success. The next day the day driver, who had the inappropriate name of Deo Gratias, said he had been 'told' where it was and took me there. It had run out of petrol and been driven into a hedge. I felt for the people whose night soil had not been removed.

The gang were frequently involved in fights, and when this happened they would go, whatever the hour, to the house of the ADC. One Christmas Eve, after Susan and I had returned from mid-night Mass and had just settled down, we were roused by lights in the garden. Our bedroom was beside the front verandah, and when the gaggle arrived at the front door I opened the bedroom window to ask what they wanted. They moved towards the window so I opened the mosquito netting window to get a better view of them. They were obviously drunk. On leaning out I saw immediately below me a dark head with a long wound running back to front. One of the gang had hit another. I told them to take the man to the hospital, about a quarter of a mile away on the other side of the boma. They were satisfied by this advice and left talking and arguing, the wounded man included. They could easily have gone to the hospital direct but they wanted to tell the ADC what had happened.

The year before my arrival a bid had been put in the annual estimates for a tanker for clearing drains and sewage tanks. To our surprise, it arrived from the UK, and was an object of delight and interest to the workforce. It was undoubtedly a great help in disagreeable jobs. After a night at the club, the head of the technical college at Arapai, just outside Soroti, returned home and went to the loo. Leaning over the loo, his false teeth fell into the bowl as he pulled the plug. He rushed out to the nearest inspection trap, only to see the teeth going on their way. They eventually landed in the septic tank. The difficulty he faced was obtaining a replacement set quickly. He would have to go to Kampala and the process would take time. He remembered the new tanker. It sucked out the contents of his septic tank and spread them on the garden for inspection. The false teeth were found, sterilised and replaced in his mouth!

One of the tasks of the township labour was to run a tree nursery to provide trees and shrubs for planting around the town. There were already a number of splendid trees – eucalyptus, mavule (a hardwood tree much used for furniture) and acacias. Some fruit trees had been planted in groves. Next to our garden were grapefruit and pawpaws; in our garden guavas and mangoes. Alongside the roads a programme of planting oleanders was under way. This, with the cut grass, made for an agreeable station. The grass cutting had its price. The Hayter mowers and the tractors which drew them were constantly breaking down.

An essential and valuable custom was the 'goat bag'. This was a fund held by the DC to pay for small items that did not fall easily into any government vote. It escaped audit. In Soroti the 'goat bag' was fed by payments received from the sale of township bullocks. There was an approved number for these animals, used for many years to pull carts and the night soil wagon. They gradually grew in number. Another way in which we kept to the approved number was to 'write off' elderly beasts to provide a feast for the township labour at Christmas.

SETTLING INTO WORK

In October 1956 all the cadets and wives attended a two-week course at the training centre at Nzamisi in Entebbe. It was intended to give us background to the situation in Uganda and to make visits to organisations, some government, others non-government. There were lectures in the morning and visits in the afternoon to such places as Makerere University, the Animal Health Institute and research stations. It was a relaxed time; we went twice to the pictures in Kampala and did some shopping, mostly for the house, which still lacked curtains. Susan, Adrian and I stayed with the families in the annex of the Lake Victoria Hotel. It was comfortable but the hotel would not allow ayahs, so looking after Adrian as well as attending the course was tiring for Susan. She had all the washing and ironing on top of the course. In those days nappies were made of material and it was essential to iron them (and clothes) on both sides to ensure that insect eggs and parasites were eliminated. The most unpleasant was mango fly. It laid an egg under the skin, which turned into a maggot which had to be squeezed out when it was sufficiently large. Until electricity arrived, the ironing was carried out with a charcoal iron with a chamber into which hot charcoal was placed. It required skill to judge the right temperature for ironing. If too hot, the clothes singed.

One night we were to meet Sir Andrew Cohen in the house of the course supervisor, Roly Peagram. We sat around his sitting room sipping our drinks carefully and not eating the sandwiches until the governor arrived. He came late from Legislative Council, greeted us, grumbled about the members of the council and at the same time quickly consumed all the sandwiches, showering crumbs over the carpet. He was frank and human, and we liked him even though, as young cadets, we were a little in awe of him.

November was an interesting month. There were riots in Lira, the chief town in the next-door district, Lango. They were instigated by the Uganda National Congress on the basis of opposition to the land tenure proposals, which were intended to address the problem of tribal as opposed to individual holdings of land in an increasingly modern economy when security – e.g. land – was needed to support loans for developing farms and businesses. Any suggestion of changes to the system of landholding was regarded with suspicion; it was 'stealing' land. Jake Jacobs, DC Lango, has described the riots in *Looking back at the Uganda Protectorate*, compiled by Douglas and Marcelle Brown. Derrick Johnson, who was an ADC in Lango at the time, has given me his recollections of the riots.

The riots consisted of the stoning of the District Council offices and then the police. Later there were disturbances in some of the outlying townships, mostly involving Asian shops. The attack on the police resulted in the reading of the Riot Act and the shooting of one of the rioters. He was only wounded. The disturbance then reduced to such activities as riding around the district headquarters on bicycles.

News of the riots came quickly to Soroti, with a request for assistance. A detachment of police under Don Robertson, who had just been married in the Native Anglican church in Soroti, Edward Cunningham and I set off for Lira. On the way there were a few places where branches had been placed on the road. They did not hold us up. Edward and I were to work in the DC's office so that the two local ADCs could tour the district. There was little to do. Edward soon returned to Soroti and I sat in the office collating reports from around the district. It was pretty boring, as the disturbances soon died down. I have a copy of one letter of appeal for help sent to the DC: 'These all fellow want to rubbed Aboke township and this morning gave us warning that when the Police will go then we will be going on rubbed. I was send our boy to cling your ear sir but they refused and told us if you send your boy for clinging ear we will kill you. Then we afraid and couldn't send out boy. These all fellow are very very danger for Aboke.' A most unpleasant situation for the sender.

I stayed with the Jacobs. It was thought right that I should wear my safari kit with brass buttons and a shoulder tab. The first day I emerged for breakfast, Jake looked at me and said: 'Look at your buttons. You're not in the merchant navy.' So polishing my buttons was my next task. In all, I was away a week with not a great deal to do.

Going to the Lira riot

The next event was the farewell tour of Sir Andrew Cohen. In Soroti it was to last three days. I had become involved earlier in a cricket match in Mbale between Mbale and the Governor's Eleven. Jim Barber, a fellow cadet, was a good cricketer. He was fielding at short leg when the governor was batting. Cohen played the ball to Jim and then moved out of his crease. Jim promptly ran him out, and then realised with horror what he had done! I remember the match mainly for Cohen's grumbling when the tea interval arrived. He wanted to go on playing. He loved his cricket.

There was another cricket match in Soroti. We beat the Governor's Eleven easily, the first defeat it had that season. I took three wickets for four runs in four balls. We put them into bat again and Cohen made forty-four which, I think, was his highest score. What tact! At a party that evening he joined the group where Susan and I were and talked cricket. Towards the end his aide-de-camp (ADC), Charles Lewis, who had been at Cambridge with Edward Cunningham, told Cohen that he was expected to make a speech. His face fell and he said he really could not, and asked the ADC to go and get him some champagne. The ADC insisted that he speak, and he did it well.

Most of the visit consisted of official openings: a farm school, technical school and Teso College, the senior secondary school with its fine buildings. There were social occasions. On 18 November, after the cricket match, a sundowner took place at the Indian Club given by Hasham Mitha, a garage owner and leading light in the Indian community (he had been awarded the MBE). Cohen also carried out the official turning on of the electricity supply to Soroti. My role, as the junior administrative officer, was to ferry various VIPs to events. It will be obvious that the junior ADC's role was to pick up the odd jobs.

The highlight of the visit was the interracial ball at Teso College. The wives on the station were expected to prepare food. This was the occasion when Salatieri's father died and he still returned to help. On the night, we arrived early to help with the last-minute details and be ready to check tickets. The Uganda Police Band was playing. The first arrivals were the Asian men, without wives. They followed their usual practice of sitting around the walls and took almost no part in the dancing. The Ugandans arrived late but came with their wives. One brought four wives on one ticket; another paid for his second wife but did not dance with her all evening. The ball, inevitably, started slowly, but gradually the Ugandans started to dance in local style, like jiving, and enjoyed it so much that they had to be persuaded at the end to stop. They would have gone on all night. A group of Europeans gave a demonstration eightsome reel, slightly spoilt by the music in the first section being played on a gramophone at twice the proper pace.

We enjoyed the dancing. Susan danced with the Governor, Tom Cox, the Provincial Commissioner, and Charles Lewis. When she was dancing with the District Education Officer he steered her near the governor and said: 'Susan, I do wish you were black!' Susan had met Lady Cohen at the cricket match and was again introduced to her at the dance: in all, she was introduced to her four times! She was not easy for a young wife to talk to but Susan was spared by the announcement of a Paul Jones (an 'excuse-me' dance during the course of which a man may change partners).

At the end of November, after the governor's visit, we all went on my first solo safari. As I wrote to my mother-in-law, Hazel Hastings, I wondered if I would get through to the people. It was a question one asked all through. I think the most one could do was to keep their attention and, most important, make them laugh. The tour was in Kumi ebuku, with a real mix of rest houses. The weather was hot during the day, the lowest temperature being 80°F. One of the problems of safari was the cold at night. This sounds odd, but the temperature, even in the dry season, dropped at night. Adrian particularly found this a problem and consequently woke very early, giving us a long day. The secret, especially for the camp beds we used, was to have as much beneath one as above.

The Church Mission Society (CMS) ran a leprosy centre just outside Kumi township. It was run by Dr Lea, who had been ordained after many years as a doctor in the UK. We visited the centre as part of the safari. A week later we returned for its discharge ceremony, which happened twice a year. It was a big occasion, because even patients who would have to return were allowed out for Christmas. There were other leper camps in the district which were visited during safaris. One became completely used to talking to people with maimed or absent hands and feet, and deformed faces. We were told that the new drugs would eliminate leprosy. However, in 1996 and 2000 Susan and I went to the big leprosy centre at Buluba, on Lake Victoria, run by Ugandan nuns. In the complex which includes a hospital, convent and farms on 800 acres, there is a Cheshire Home for burnt-out cases who cannot return to the community. Leprosy can take many years to emerge, and we were told that its transmission is still not fully understood. Some 1,000 new cases are identified each year, many from areas without a history of leprosy. Mercifully, modern drugs are able to control the condition. But it is far from disappearing.

The only other event in November was the arrival of my mother's Chappell baby grand. It was in terrible condition, the keyboard frame cracked and twisted, even though it had been surrounded with a mattress and two carpets. Luckily, insurance paid, so we were able to get someone, a highly competent Sikh from Nairobi, to repair it.

SOCIAL LIFE

Our first months in Soroti were made easier, especially for Susan, by the support we received from other residents, both government and commercial, the latter mostly employed by the banks. During my absence in Lira Susan wrote to her mother:

> Everyone here is awfully nice to me, offering to have me to meals and even to stay. But I am staying here alone partly because I don't want to move Adrian and partly because I have just got to get used to it – this is just the first of many separations.

Susan was homesick during our first Christmas, missing her family, particularly her mother, and the kind of family Christmas she had enjoyed in Oxford.

I did miss you so much over Christmas, everyone but especially you. I felt terribly alien to everyone here, their idea of Christmas being so different from my own; and I find the quantities of alcohol that drift about rather overwhelming. Anyway I'd have given a lot to be a millionaire and fly home for those days.

Mrs Hastings sent money, which arrived before Christmas and enabled us to buy a radio. Many of the parcels from the UK coming by ship did not arrive on time. Others, including a plate and mug for Adrian from my parents, had been badly packed and arrived broken.

The range of entertainments in Soroti was limited. There were plenty of parties and sport but the few films were usually provided by Shell or the British Council. On one memorable night we watched *The Three Musketeers* with the reels out of order. The centre of our social life was the Soroti Club. It was open to Europeans only; there were almost no Ugandans in senior positions. The only one I remember was the deputy to the District Medical Officer (DMO). So, during our time in Soroti, the problem did not arise of whether to admit Ugandans as members. The club was much used by members and their families. After games – tennis, squash or golf – it was the place to go and have a drink. After the children were in bed we would often go there, leaving Ludya to look after them. There were dances and celebrations. The committee ran it well, employing an excellent Ugandan barman. In 1957 the club decided to build its own swimming pool. Sterling Astaldi were constructing the new road between Mbale and Soroti. They agreed to dig the hole. Officials in the PWD (Public Works Department) supervised the construction of the concrete pool and its surround. A small, shallow pool for children was at one end. It was a great day when the water was put in and we were able to add swimming to the pleasures of the weekend.

We had one scare with Adrian in the shallow pool. Susan was talking to another wife and by chance looked at Adrian. He was on his back with his face going under water. He was trying to get upright but his heels were slipping on the bottom. Susan grabbed him and turned him upside down, and he coughed up lots of water. Following this incident he would not put his head into the water, which made learning to swim difficult.

There were many social events. On Christmas Eve there was a children's party at the Soroti Club, with Father Christmas arriving to dispense presents in a trailer drawn by a township tractor. In the evening a group went round the station (the government and senior commercial houses) singing carols. We then went to a quiet midnight Mass. On Christmas Day, after pre-lunch drinks with the DC and his wife, we took our turkey, sausages and wine to the house of the District Medical Officer, Keith Batten, and had lunch with him and his wife, Pat. After lunch some of us went to swim in the almost derelict pool down by the swampy area beyond the government housing. It was an unattractive place, where I saw a cobra slide from below me into the water beyond the pool. There was another pool at the Agricultural Experimental Station at Serere a few miles from Soroti, which we also used until the club built its own pool. On Boxing Day a men versus women cricket match was held. It was light-hearted, with absurd penalties. Susan made six runs but was fined five for threatening me, the bowler, with no lunch. The scorer thought she had been given more runs so she was recorded with eleven. You can picture the scene. After the cricket there was another swim. It was a very hot time. Barrie Bleach, a master at Teso College, stayed with us over Christmas. At the club party on Christmas Eve, Barrie won a pig's head. When we returned from midnight Mass, the head greeted us in a bowl in the kitchen sink. At New Year the club held a fancy dress dance. Susan went in a sari and I as a file. Then, to Susan's delight, the parcels from the UK arrived.

Sport was an important element of Soroti life. Near the club were tennis courts and a squash court (still being used in 1996). There were regular tennis competitions, which pleased Susan as tennis was her game. For me there was an endless round of games: hockey, with Asians forming much of Soroti's team; cricket, again with many Asians in the team. The cricket and hockey matches, usually against teams from other districts, took place at the (interracial) Soroti Sports Club;

tennis at the club. I was sports secretary of the Soroti Sports Club and the club. All this took much of my time, and as Susan commented tartly: '[A]nd on top of all this, there is the minor little point of his job, not to mention his family.' A typical away game took place at the end of January 1957. On most occasions we would stay away overnight. On this occasion we went to Lira, a round trip of 166 miles, where I played hockey in the morning and evening. One took such trips for granted but they could be tiring on murram roads, with, in the dry season, their dust. When she arrived in Uganda Susan could not drive, so she had learnt under my instruction – not ideal for family harmony. She took her test in 1957 with the examiner coming from Gulu. She failed but passed the second time towards the end of 1957, when heavily pregnant with Nicholas.

I was not a golfer though both Susan and I played occasionally. The nine-hole course was slightly eccentric. Most of the tees were the usual platforms but the course had a scattering of low rocky outcrops, miniature versions of Soroti Rock. One of the rocks had a level area some 15 ft up. It was highly enjoyable to tee up looking right down the fairway from one's eyrie. The other curious feature, at least when compared with courses in temperate climates, was its hardness during the dry season. A well-struck drive would bounce for an enormous distance.

The dances, especially the fancy dress, were great fun, and considerable effort went into the costumes. The arrival of Susan's mother helped us; she was a marvellous needlewoman. For New Year 1957, shortly before Susan had Nicholas, I went in one of her maternity dresses as a very pregnant lady. At dances an immense amount of alcohol was drunk. One has to bear in mind the climate, as alcohol was sweated out very quickly. On one occasion the Barclays Bank manager, Tubby Pearce, came as Batman. He looked splendid. By the end of the dance he was asleep on the ground outside, and so deeply that a cigarette burnt a mark on his chest without waking him. Despite the drinking I cannot recall one official who allowed club visits to interfere with his work.

SHOPPING

There was a well-established routine for shopping in Soroti. It was assumed that for any but the most common supplies and articles one went to Kampala. In Soroti one bought the basics of living. The range of produce was greatly increased when the railway reached Soroti, early in our tour. There were deliveries twice a week from Kenya, so we were able to order milk, which arrived in tetrapaks. Vegetables could also be ordered from Kenya. Otherwise food was bought locally. The grocer Susan patronised was Nazareth Brothers, run by two Goan brothers who attended church, as we did, in the Goan Institute. They had a good stock but were expensive. We settled their bill once a month. The market was a source of good meat. Fin Haddock, the District Veterinary Officer, was encouraging the butchers to produce proper cuts of meat instead of lumps hacked from a carcass. Fin's success meant that Susan was able to buy delicious steaks at a remarkably low price as all meat was the same price.

My clothes, khaki shorts and safari jacket, were made to measure by a local Asian tailor, Mohanlal Ghelabhai. Two pairs of shorts cost EAShs 14 and two safari jackets EAShs 120 (20 shs to £1). He also

Soroti Club, 1957

supplied us with clothes for the servants. A khanzu, a long overgarment reaching to the ankles, cost EAShs 17. Another of the first essential purchases were calf-length leather mosquito boots, brown for Susan and black for me, to protect our ankles from mosquito bites, especially on safari. They were measured by us placing our feet on a piece of paper. Well made, they finally collapsed when worn by our children in the UK. Long trousers and long-sleeved shirts buttoned at the wrist were also essential to reduce the area for mosquitoes to attack. At first our car was serviced, and we bought our petrol from the Shell garage run by Hasham Metha. Later we transferred our custom to the Star service station (Caltex) run by Dharas and his sons. Looking through our bills shows that it was possible to obtain all one's necessities in Soroti from well-run shops and businesses. It was no surprise many years later to read that a Uganda Asian, one of the mass of Asians expelled by Idi Amin, had won the UK garage of the year award.

In December I had my first experience of a county show. It combined the parading of animals with a feast and dancing. This one took place in Bukedea, an ebuku in the south of Teso. The dance started with the drums being heated to the right pitch by holding them over a small fire. Often it was the women who struck the drums. While the dancing was starting the chiefs and elders would retire to a temporary hut to drink the local beer. This was made of fermented millet placed in a pot onto which hot water was poured. This warm beer was sucked up a long tube made from vine stems. At the end in the pot was a piece of open gauze to prevent pieces of the beer going up the tube and blocking it. Warm beer sounds unpleasant, but I liked it. If a large number were drinking from the pot, there would be two rows. Those near the pot had short tubes; those further away long ones.

SAFARI

In early January 1957 we went for three days of safari to Ngora county on the road south to Mbale. The ebuku rest house was luxurious, a permanent building with two bedrooms, so Adrian had a room to himself. Behind the rest house was Ngora Rock, a smaller version of Soroti Rock, with rock paintings, mostly spirals. Ngora township was dominated by two large missions, Church Mission Society and Catholic. I visited the Freda Carr Hospital, run by the CMS. It was full of pneumonia and dysentery patients, typical for the dry season. Most patients had been joined by their families, who stayed in huts at the edge of the hospital compound, cooked their food and generally cheered up the patients, who, if well enough, would join them in the compound. When the hospital first opened families were allowed to stay in the wards. The result was chaos, with families, bicycles and even goats blocking the way. So they were banished. In the operating theatre we met a former member of Mau Mau who was working, most efficiently, as a dresser. There was also a maternity ward for twenty-two, but it was often overfull with mothers-to-be sleeping on the floor. The mothers stayed four days after birth unless there were complications. The Catholic hospital was for maternity cases, again about twenty-two. It was not so well equipped but was efficiently run. When I moved

The dancing beginning

The feast begins, Bukedea County Show

from Ngora rest house Susan returned to Soroti, as the next two rest houses were in poor condition.

Back in Soroti we heard that the contract for wiring the government houses had been let and was expected to be completed in fourteen weeks.

The usual routine of safari needs to be described. Salatieri would bring a cup of tea and hot water for shaving at 7.30 a.m. After dressing in safari kit (the safari jacket had one shoulder flash for an ADC, two for a DC and three for a PC), it was wonderful to stand outside the rest house in the early morning and smell the fresh earth and the smoke from the kitchen and nearby homesteads. Even in the dry season in Teso, the mornings had freshness. After a substantial breakfast I would aim to be at the etem headquarters by 8.30 and at the parish (eitella) to be toured by 9.00. The tour was carried out either on foot or, if the country was flat, on a bicycle. The choice of village was made by the chiefs. They tended to select one nearby. After a number of tours in the ebuku it was possible to demand to visit a more remote and less visited village. In these it was possible to make a

Bushman paintings in a cave on Ngora Rock
just above the town of Ngora

Salatieri supervising Juma at Atetur rest camp

more realistic assessment of the state of the etem and the effectiveness of its chiefs.

The tour would be lead by the eitella chief followed by myself, the interpreter, the ebuku and etem chiefs and various elders. At each house we would be greeted by the owner and taken round the homestead, which had been tidied for the visit. It was only in the most remote homes near the Karamoja border or, later, in Ankole, in homes away over the hills, that scruffiness was not always disguised. The purpose of the visit was to ensure that the homesteads were clean, the lavatories were constructed in accordance with the health by-laws and that each household had a famine reserve of grain (millet), again required by law. The reserve was held in mud and wattle constructions with grass roofs, like miniature huts. The difference was that the reserve stood on legs to keep the grain off the ground. The requirement arose from famines in the 1940s and was strictly enforced. The aim was to grow enough to fill a new reserve store each year. The oldest reserve could then be used.

The lavatory inspection was always good value. I tried to discover whether the pit was at least six feet deep. It was a slog to dig deep in areas where there was murram. I would drop a stone through the hole in the ground into the pit. If the noise of the stone hitting the bottom was slightly delayed, the pit was deep enough; if the noise was instantaneous, the lavatory was ornamental. The discovery of a fraud would cause much laughter at the expense of the owner, who would be instructed to comply with the regulations. I wonder if they ever did.

After the visit, which might include a primary school, a rural dispensary, a recently constructed 'tank' for storing rainwater or an agricultural improvement scheme, I would hold a meeting, sometimes at the etem headquarters but more often in the area which had been visited. The villagers who had been rounded up to attend the meeting would sit on the ground, with the elders on chairs. The chiefs and I would sit facing them. These meetings were of twenty to thirty people; those at the headquarters would attract more. I would then give items of national news and explain government policy on, for example,

Ngino rest camp on our first safari

coming elections. The meeting would then be addressed by the ebuku chief. Question time followed, the most enjoyable part of the meeting. There were always catch questions raised by the same questioners. The object was to get a new ADC to give a wrong answer. One quickly learnt to recognise such questions and consult the ebuku chief. Often there were genuine problems which needed to be resolved: law cases, pensions, tax assessment. Occasionally there were government policies which aroused interest and sometimes, anger. Land tenure was always tricky. The increased population and the pressure it created on the land was reflected in the number of cases involving land in the courts. This led to efforts to establish a more permanent system of holding land. The result in Teso was uproar. The government was 'stealing' their land. The Iteso were an attractive people, straightforward in saying what they thought. This resulted in some lively meetings.

Sometimes these meetings were ill-attended and therefore dreary. The part of Teso on the shore of Lake Kioga, in ebuku Serere, where the fishermen were a busy and close-knit community, was the worst. It was also an area where bhang was widely smoked. It had an atmosphere of determined backwardness, or at least determination to be different.

In my early tours I used to return to the rest camp for lunch before going to the etem headquarters to inspect its books. This was not satisfactory, as the chiefs had to wait until I returned and then work later than necessary. I therefore worked straight through, eating when the work was finished. So lunch was anytime between 15.00 and 18.00 depending on the size of the etem.

At the etem headquarters I would check the sub-county court records to ensure that decisions were in line with the law. A common offence in Teso was cattle theft. It would take place because cattle were wealth, useful in their own right but also as a means of paying the bride price for a wife. The standard punishment was two years in jail and six strokes with a cane. The former held no terrors; the latter was much disliked. The tax receipts would then be checked against the tax tickets issued to ensure that the entries in the cash book and cash balance were accurate. Counting tax tickets and cash at the height of the tax season took time. Often old men were presented for Poll Tax exemption on the simple grounds that old men who could not work could not pay. In such cases one always consulted the chief.

It was usual to spend one day in each etem on the basic safari work. A second day could be spent on special tasks, such as inspecting the border area between Teso and Karamoja after there had been cattle raids and killings. The final day of a tour would be spent at the ebuku headquarters. This was a more formal occasion and consisted of checking the court records, original cases and appeals from etem courts, checking the cash and tax returns and sometimes visiting a district government prison. The prison visit included an inspection of the buildings, checking the records to ensure the correct release dates had been recorded (and that no one was being held improperly) and to hear complaints. Only rarely were there errors in the release dates, either to the advantage or disadvantage of prisoners, and I can only remember one occasion when a prisoner had been held too long. While checking the release dates, all the prisoners appeared before me, when they had an opportunity to make a complaint. Most were about

In safari dress, Atetur rest camp, November 1956

the food. There were also requests for help over domestic problems. One curious case was that of a young hermaphrodite. When it was his turn to come before me, there was some amusement. I asked what it was about and was told. He/she had no complaints.

Teso District Council was responsible for a number of prisons. One was just outside Soroti. The ebuku chief was elderly and did not take much interest in the running of the prison, rarely visiting it. One day a prisoner was found hanging on a tree away from the prison. It was suicide, but the obvious question was how he got there. I was instructed by the DC to conduct an enquiry. I interviewed the chief, warders and some of the prisoners. It quickly emerged that prisoners were allowed out at weekends on an unofficial basis. In fact, they could come and go at will. The unfortunate man who had hanged himself had domestic problems which became too much for him. The proximity of Soroti ebuku to Soroti meant that it was visited more often by departmental officers who had no responsibility for checking the prison, and was not high on the priorities of the DC and his staff. More distant ibukui (counties) needed our attention. Following my inquiry, the prison rules were tightened. The ebuku chief retired not long after this affair, and it was decided to tour the ebuku more frequently.

The final act of the safari was to give the ebuku chief one's assessment of the tour and to discuss with him any problems he might have and his views on policy matters. Most ebuku chiefs were of high quality. Some of the older ones were idle. In one case a powerful ebuku chief tried to take over control of the District Council and its committees, relying on his local support in Kaberamaido. He was dismissed by the Governor. The younger ebuku chiefs were well educated and spoke good English. One dealt with them as one government servant to another.

Each county had a tour book. At the end of each day it was important to make entries under each heading, such as chiefs, courts, health. It was possible looking back over the years to get a very good idea of the character of an ebuku or etem, the effectiveness of its chiefs and the developments which had taken place. I wonder what has happened to these tour books, as they are a valuable primary source for researchers.

It was marvellous after a long, hot day to return to the rest camp for a late tea and a bath in the canvas bath bought from Walters. When

Adrian came on safari, his evening bath outside the rest house was an entertainment watched by women and children. The late afternoon sounds – the voices from the nearby homes, the call of birds and the feeling of the day slowing down towards evening – were soothing and relaxing. After the bath I would get into long trousers, a long-sleeved shirt buttoned at the wrist and the mosquito boots. Then a bottle of beer before supper. In the more remote camps there would be a fire, on the edge of the compound. As the evening got cooler it was a pleasure to sit by the fire, listening to the evening sounds of nearby homes, insects and the occasional animal. The fire also kept mosquitoes away.

1957: SICKNESS AND LOCAL LEAVE

In early February 1957 we took our first break, a few days in the Murchison Falls Park. Mary Watson, the wife of Arthur Watson, the ADC1, had undertaken to look after Adrian. We spent a night in the rest house in Gulu and then went on to Paraa Lodge in the park, where we were joined by Bill Clarence, who had been posted to Kitgum, a sub-district of Acholi. John Savage, the warden, looked after us. We went to the head of the Murchison (now Kabarega) Falls, where the Nile, a hundred yards wide at the top, drops through a narrow channel to the river below. We saw the more common game but failed to see any rhino. John told us that some of the scenes for the film *Magambo* had been shot in the park. One required the hero, played by Clark Gable, to swim across the river. He declined to do so. In the confidence of youth and despite the crocodiles, John volunteered. He said that, by the end of the swim, the crocs were getting close! His fee was £5.

In mid-February I was again on safari, this time in ebuku Usuku in the north of the district. It was a different kind of country bordering on Karamoja. It was mainly open savannah, with thorn and acacia trees. It was the target for cross-border cattle raids by the Karamojong. I enjoyed touring there.

In Soroti the wiring of houses came to a premature stop. Before the first house was completed, the Public Works Department had run out of plugs and wall lamp fittings.

In February the DC's secretary went on three weeks' leave and Susan took over. She worked mainly on a report for the new Governor, Sir Frederick Crawford. The rush meant her working late into the night, though she was allowed a break at teatime to see Adrian and do her stint at the library in the club.

The wiring of our house had begun by now but the wiring programme continued to stagger along. This time there was a shortage of water heaters. Some houses had one in the kitchen, others one in the bathroom. We had neither. Fortunately for everyone's tempers, some rain came at the end of January. The grass quickly turned green and flowers came to life. One variety in the garden had bluebell-shaped flowers. The growth appeared in the morning; by teatime there were buds like unopened daffodils; by evening the flowers were open.

At the end of January Adrian had had a short bout of malaria. One night his temperature had been over 104°F. At one in the morning he had a screaming fit for half an hour. Then, at the beginning of March, he developed an upset tummy. He had a good breakfast and was taken out, as usual, by Ludya to play with the other children. He refused to play and just wanted to lie down. Ludya brought him home and he was put to bed. He had developed a temperature. It was a Saturday, and I was due to be received into the Roman Catholic Church on Sunday. After lunch Adrian had a short rest, and after he had woken I cradled him in my arms while Susan went to get some medicine. Adrian then went into convulsions and was very white and limp. We rushed him to the house of the District Medical Officer, Keith Batten. He immediately sent me to collect the senior Nursing Sister, Althea Goldsmith. Luckily, she was at home. Keith had already taken Adrian into the bathroom, and when Althea arrived I think they plunged him into a cold bath (we were rightly excluded). Keith also gave him a large dose of an anti-malarial drug. Adrian came out of his convulsions but Keith, who thought he had cerebral malaria, said he should be taken to Nakasero Hospital in Kampala. Keith would accompany us. The shortest route involved crossing on the Awoja ferry (the bridge had not yet been built). So Owen Griffith drove to the ferry to hold it ready. We arrived at the hospital at 10.30 at night. The next day Adrian appeared better and Keith returned to Soroti.

Susan remained a week in Nakasero looking after Adrian and the other children, three girls aged six, three and one, in the ward. The first night Susan was up most of the night administering to them, so by six in the morning, when the nurse came in to take temperatures and wake everyone, Susan was exhausted. I had stayed the night with an American couple, the Burkes, who were attached to Makerere University. The Burkes invited Susan to lunch. With the doctor's agreement she took Adrian so that he could have a sleep. She took him back at teatime. Adrian had received no treatment that day and was obviously developing another high temperature. On their return to Nakasero the Nursing Sisters – part-time and not apparently much interested in the patients – made it clear that they thought Susan irresponsible for taking Adrian out, and the final straw came when the night sister remarked in the early hours, when Adrian was screaming, that Susan had treated the hospital as an hotel and could give Adrian his medicine herself. Daphne Burke was also 'sleeping' in the hospital, as her three-year-old daughter was very unwell and had to be given injections every six hours. The night sister also made unpleasant comments about Daphne and her daughter, reducing her to tears. In the early hours Daphne went home to feed her month-old baby and tell Fred Burke what had happened. At six Fred arrived to do battle. He told the doctor what he thought of the way his daughter, Becky, and his wife had been treated. Later Susan added her complaints. The doctor was understanding, and care improved in the ward. It was cleaned and a nurse turned up from time to time. More importantly the doctor began to explain the treatment that Adrian was receiving, but Susan still had to feed the children and try to keep them amused. The basic problem in the hospital was a shortage of staff.

By Monday Susan was a wreck. I stayed with Adrian so she could go to the Burkes, sleep and wash the nappies. Adrian improved through the week, and on Thursday we went back to Soroti, stopping for lunch at the Barbers in Jinja and for tea with John Kaboha in Mbale. Did Adrian really have cerebral malaria? The doctors could not agree. One thought he had; another doubted it but could not suggest what had struck him. Luckily, Adrian had no recurrences, but it meant that Susan and the children could only occasionally go on safari with me. The risk of malaria was too great.

The electricity saga continued. In mid-March electricity was three houses away and the supply wires connected to our house. We had received a cooker and one water heater. The DC and his wife had been a month out of their house to allow it to be wired. The D.M.O's house had a disaster. The workmen had removed some pipes from a tank in the roof without draining it, with the result that a bedroom and bathroom were flooded. The workmen were just walking away when the DMO's wife, Pat, made them return to do something about the mess.

At the end of March electricity arrived. The workmen, unsurprisingly, made a mess. They coincided with Adrian going down with tonsillitis – which, to our dismay, was initially diagnosed as malaria – and the arrival of the new Governor. As the township ADC I had been making sure the place looked attractive. My special care was directed to the golf course, as the governor was a keen golfer. An outdoors sundowner was given in the DC's garden. We were a little apprehensive, as the proper rains were due. A letter from Susan to her mother described the occasion:

> Pat came back at tea time. Adrian had to lie on him instead of me and I had to rush off and help the DC's wife prepare the party in HE's honour. All this time the workmen were banging away in our house and the mess was getting worse and worse but somehow we got a screaming Adrian to bed, pushed the workmen out of the house and changed for the party in a quarter of an hour, walking over huge bits of wall that had been pulled down and trying to find

a dress out of cupboards turned back to front, if you know what I mean. Anyhow we made it.

Sir Frederick Crawford was a complete contrast to Sir Andrew Cohen. Crawford came with a reputation of being prepared to listen. In appearance he was impeccably dressed, and he was polite; I saw him rise quickly to light the cigarette of one of the women guests. Cohen would not have noticed; he always looked a bit of a mess and could be rude. Lady Crawford came with the reputation of being a grumbler. On this tour she had reached Mbale but refused to continue the tour. However, she had been bitten by the DC's dog in Mbale; not tactful.

In April the electricians finished, so redecoration could begin. Enough rooms were painted to allow the Barbers, now in Mbale, and John Kaboha to stay. We took them to Karamoja for a picnic tea. While the redecoration continued the carpenters arrived to replace the woodwork of the verandah, which had been badly eaten by termites. On 13 April I was, at last, received into the Roman Catholic Church, at the Madera mission, by Bishop Grief. On 4 May we went on our first two weeks' local leave to Kenya. We drove to Tororo and turned left onto the Nairobi road. The first night was spent in the Highlands Hotel in Molo. It was marvellous, after the dryness and heat of Soroti, to go into the highlands, with their greenness and flowers and the blissful cool. We then visited bank friends in Nakuru, passing through country I knew as a boy, and arrived in Nairobi to stay with Barclays Bank friends.

We also stayed with friends of my parents, the Boyds, in Limuru. They had a fruit farm and canning factory. Between the wars they had developed the farm and built a most attractive house, with stunning views over the lush countryside of Limuru. They spoke of the situation during the Mau Mau emergency, when they had continued to run the farm. They were told by the police that their houseboy was secretary of the local Mau Mau gang. When the emergency was over the Boyds asked him whether he would have killed them if ordered to do so. He said he would not have done so but had an arrangement with a Mau Mau servant working for neighbours, the Kingsfords, that they would each kill the other's employers. The houseboy had settled back into the Boyds' household. They had another case which illustrated in an awful way the effect of tribal beliefs. One of their staff became sick and did not seem to be getting better. Boyd talked to him and was told that he was sick as a result of a curse on him. Boyd urged him to get up and try to work but without success. The sick man just turned his face to the wall and died.

I think it might give a flavour of the rush of life in Soroti if I described two months: June and July 1957. On our return at the end of May from leave in Kenya, Susan discovered she had become secretary of Soroti Red Cross. She had also been elected 'house member' of the club, which would involve organising at Whitsun a tea and a dance on the Saturday and lunch and tea on the Sunday. The redecoration of the house was continuing and Susan knew she was pregnant with our second child.

1 June was Commonwealth Day, so I was sent to an ebuku headquarters – I think Kumi – to read the Queen's speech, add a few words of my own and take a march past of the assembled young, mostly scouts and guides. I disliked reading or making speeches on these occasions and felt for those who had to listen to them. They must have seemed remote from their lives. However, those taking part showed every sign of enjoying the occasion, especially the march past with the band playing. I think it was one of those occasions when we drip-fed peoples' minds with the concept of the Commonwealth as a group of nations bound together by common links. Later I was surprised, when Director General of the Security Service, to realise that during the course of liaison visits, and especially at Commonwealth security conferences, there was a bond which made such events agreeable and occasionally profitable. The British colonial background was a link, and despite political problems there was an inclination on such occasions to look to the UK for a lead.

The Whitsun festivities included a tennis tournament in which Owen Griffith and I won the doubles. The Uganda Cricket Association visited for a couple of matches. Soroti lost badly to them. Susan organised the meals, though suffering from morning sickness. The next weekend the Health Inspector, who was about to go on leave, gave a party and there was a childrens' party at the club. Another cadet of our year and his wife, the Barnes, stayed. One of the most attractive traditions of colonial life was the hospitality one received wherever one went. The government rest houses at district headquarters were used but for the most part someone would offer a bed and meal. This applied whether one was on leave or visiting for the weekend for a cricket or hockey or golf match.

In mid-June the Griffiths' new son, Michael, was christened in the picturesque mud and wattle and thatched Anglican church in Soroti. I had what was described as a congested liver and had to take masses of glucose. In late June I was away again on safari, which allowed me some free time to study for the obligatory law exams. It was a condition of confirmation as a District Officer that one had to pass the local law exams and two languages at lower level. I did pass the law exams at the end of June (thereby qualifying to be a third-class magistrate) and then turned to learning Ateso (all the cadets had passed lower Luganda at Oxford). Ateso is not an easy language, especially for people such as myself without a gift for languages. A few administrative officers mastered it or the related Akaramojong. One was John Brasnett, who passed it at higher level. My tutor was Father Hilders, a Mill Hill Father, who had written with a former Teso DC, Jerry Lawrence, an introduction to Ateso, which I used in my studies. I also used the Ateso–English and English–Ateso dictionaries compiled by another Mill Hill priest, Father Kiggen. It must have been agony for Father Hilders to teach me, but he was patient and I eventually passed lower Ateso on 26 January 1959.

I had handed over responsibility for the Soroti labour and its associated work to a more junior ADC from the new influx of cadets arriving a year after us. The one sent to Soroti was billeted on us until his house was ready, but it was not a success. Our house was too small to have an extra person. So he went and shared with a young police cadet.

One of my areas of work was gun licences. All applications had to be approved by the DC. My job was to ensure that all applications had been processed properly. This meant support from the ebuku chief and clearance by the senior police officer in the district. One had to be sure that the person was someone of standing in the community who was unlikely to misuse the gun. Normally licences were only given for shotguns. Anyone permitted to hold a rifle had to obtain a game licence for larger animals, such as elephant.

Another activity was accompanying the police, as a magistrate, when they carried out raids for illicit stills making waragi, a powerful spirit which could fetch a decent price. This involved getting up early in the morning and searching every house in the chosen area. Sleepy households were woken and buildings searched. Often stills were found and the owners arrested.

In July the Entebbe Club visited for a cricket weekend. Soroti lost badly to them. We put up one of the team and Susan organised tea and a party in the evening. Inevitably, Adrian was sick; this time he had a boil on his leg and vomiting. The rains had arrived at last, and there were storms with heavy rain and lightning. At the end of July I was again on safari. Then preparations began for a big social occasion: the Scott (golf) Cup over the August bank holiday weekend. We had friends to stay.

Susan had been given a morning job as a shorthand typist in the DC's office. She was responsible for some of the confidential work. When she was working for the DC, the DC's office was visited by the Special Branch officer from Mbale. He spent time reading the safari reports and taking notes from them. They appeared to form the basis of some of his reports. This sounds slightly absurd, but I suppose it shows the extent of the coverage that Administrative Officers had of the district. Susan also worked for the D.M.O., the District Education Officer and an agricultural officer when they needed typing to be done. These jobs helped to pay off the car. In April Miss Thompson, my former governess, had lent us £600 to pay off the government loan on our car. My father agreed to pay her interest and we repaid her

£25 a month. Later, my father took over the loan from her and we paid him instead. Ludya went into hospital at this time; she was continuing to suffer from gynaecological problems.

In July an important Muslim marriage took place in Soroti. We attended the third day of celebrations. The women were dressed in what Susan described as 'marvellous sugary and flimsy saris' decorated in gold. The large house was full of children, many asleep on the floor, over whom we stepped on our way to the bride. I also attended a sundowner given by two Indians, Hindus this time. They had sought Susan's advice about sandwiches as they had enjoyed the sandwiches she had provided for cricket teas.

In August the district sports events were held. They included a marathon run from the Amuria county headquarters to Soroti. Some of the runners were staggering by the end, something which the spectators, to my distress, found entertaining. Athletics had caught the interest of the district as two of Uganda's Commonwealth Games team were Iteso. One, Patrick Etolu, won a bronze medal in the high jump.

VISIT OF THE AGA KHAN

The Aga Khan, newly installed as the leader of the Ismaeli community after the death of his grandfather, visited Soroti, an important Ismaeli centre, at the end of October 1957. He was to stay in the Watsons' house. Arthur Watson was acting DC while Owen Griffith was on home leave in the UK. The reason for this arrangement was a rivalry between two prominent members of the Asian community: Hasham Metha, who ran a long-established garage, and Aziz Metha. They could not agree where he would stay. The solution sidestepped the problem.

In mid-September Susan was told that she would meet the Aga Khan when he arrived and have coffee with him and Mary Watson. Our coffee cups were to be used. Early in October we were told that our coffee cups were too elegant; bigger cups were needed. Susan was still to meet the Aga Khan. By late October Susan was out of the coffee

120

party. A degree of confusion surrounded the visit as no one knew whether his mother, Princess Joan (later Tajudula) Ali Khan, and other members of his family were to accompany him.

The excitement, particularly in the Ismaeli community, was enormous. Any article used by the Aga Khan was considered blessed. There were stories of the old Aga Khan's bath water being bottled. Inevitably, members of the community tried to place articles of their own in the Watsons' house, particularly the Aga Khan's bedroom. When the Ismaelis turned up with articles for the house, such as blankets and lights, the Watsons' houseboy asked them if they thought 'his bwana' could not afford such things!

The Aga Khan was to fly to Soroti. Who were to form the welcoming party? The acting DC, obviously; the others, together with their wives, were the Chief Superintendent of police, the D.M.O. and the head of the Public Works Department, Bert Muddle, who was a senior and long-serving member of that department. There was no one from the commercial community. The rains had come and Soroti was cooler. On the day the sun shone. The welcoming party lined up. Hovering in the background was Mackay Imlah, the manager of the Soroti branch of the Standard Bank, immaculate in a blazer. As the Aga Khan stepped from his plane, Imlah surged forward and greeted the Aga Khan, who then moved on to the official party. There was great amusement when the story reached the rest of the European community.

The visit passed off smoothly. There was a dinner in the DC's garden. The Aga Khan was charming, polite and judged good-looking. He had a good social touch, embracing the Ismaelis and shaking hands with the British officials. His retinue included a decorative Indian secretary and a British ADC.

TESO–KARAMOJA BORDER

The Iteso were farmers who both grew crops and raised cattle. Cattle were wealth and an important element in their social life, as they were used for bride price payments. The Karamojong were solely cattle people and also saw themselves as warriors. Young men expected to 'blood' their spears and acquire cattle to pay bride price. Under local laws they were only allowed to carry one spear, sufficient for hunting. Two could indicate aggressive intent. The result was much cattle raiding between the tribal groups in Karamoja, and between the tribes such as the Suk across the Kenya border, and the Karamojong. In ebuku Usuku on the Karamoja border the countryside was open savannah and sparsely occupied. Iteso homesteads were protected against raids by thick and high palisades of wood and thorn. The Karamojong looked down on the Iteso as cultivators and considered them and their cattle as fair game. The raiding reached such a pitch that it compelled the government to take action. A road was made along the border to enable the police to patrol and respond to raids more quickly. A spotter plane was also used and, each side of the border, a cordon sanitaire established which was closed to the herding of cattle.

As the ADC who mainly toured Usuku, I became involved. In mid-December 1957 I had just returned from a two-week safari. Reports came in of a raid, so the next day, a Saturday, I left at 4.00 with a young Inspector of police and some Constables to visit the scene. We met the eitella chief and drove across country following the route taken by the raiders. We soon came to the body of a man which had already been part eaten by vultures. We told the constables to place him on a blanket and put him in the Land-Rover for returning to his village. They did so with reluctance. Closer to the border, there were two other bodies which had been partly burnt. In one homestead a woman had been speared. It was a distressing sight, as she sat where she had been killed with the spear sticking out of her lower abdomen.

The local people said there had been a fight and that some of the Karamojong had been injured. However, it was agreed that, so many hours after the raid, it would be fruitless to chase the raiders, as they would be back in Karamoja and well away from the border. Their ability to travel long distances at speed even when injured was legendary.

In order to reduce the risk of raids, the law against grazing near the district border was applied rigorously. As I had passed my law exams and become a third-class magistrate, I was sent occasionally to hear cases in which trespass had taken place. I would sit at a table under a tree with an interpreter and some Native Authority (NA) police armed with .303 rifles (almost certainly not loaded). The NA police would bring the herdsman who was alleged to have grazed his herd in the closed area. The police would present their evidence; the accused would give his version of events. Often they made no excuse. The standard penalty was the forfeiture of 10% of his herd for sale at the government compound just across the border into Karamoja. It was understood that the most treasured beasts would not be seized.

1958: POLITICS, LOCAL LEAVE

So far I have said little about the political scene. My involvement as a new cadet was at this stage minimal. The District Council Ordinance of 1955 had given more powers to the district council, but relations

Usuku homestead (photo: Edward Cunningham)

with the Teso District Council were a matter for the DC and, occasionally, the ADC1. My contacts with Teso District Council officials were from ebuku chief downwards. However, like all cadets I was interested in the general political situation, partly for its own sake and, much less, for the implications for my future. Although we had been told by the chief secretary, Charles Hartwell, during the Nsamizi course that we would be able to have our full careers as Administrative Officers, we did not believe that such a long career in Uganda was possible. I cannot remember being fussed by this. There was a great deal of interesting work and the future could look after itself.

My views at the time were set out in a letter to my mother-in-law.

> The whole future of Africa is so uncertain and the air of sloth and complacency in the civil service depresses me a lot. Despite the talk of great movement to self-government here, there seems to be no definite policy in government at all. It seems to be an attitude of waiting until the local politicians make a move and then basing action on that. The result will be that self-government will be on us before either the government are prepared or the political parties have had any real experience of administration and leadership. I think it is correct to say that there is no political party with a genuine desire to face the practical problems of self-government. The political leaders are doing too well privately to want to face the economic future of a country facing the first deficit for years. The parties vie with each other for who can about for self government sooner but lose support among the people because of the dishonesty of the officials of local branches of the parties. I doubt if there are more than six African ADCs and this in a country that claims to be on the verge of self-government. Civil servants realise here just how far Uganda is away from self-government and talk glibly of us still being here in thirty years time, but I am sure that external pressure alone will force us to grant self-government at a much sooner date than that. There is a lot of 'not in my time' thinking. There are obviously some good things about Uganda but I can see some terrible difficulties ahead.

These were not very coherent comments but there was a core of truth in them. It did not occur to me at the time that independence was to be only five years away.

Through most of my time in Teso the district political scene was dominated by a dispute between the ibukui in the north of Teso, the Iseera, led by Enosi Ejoku, and the three southern ibukui, the Ingoratuk, led by N. Esunyet who came from Nyero, ebuku Kumi. It centred on the District Council Appointments Committee, which had the power to appoint chiefs. The District Council elections had resulted in changes to the Appointments Committee membership, allowing the Iseera to have a majority. They exploited it by putting their nominees into all the vacant positions. As a result, the Ingoratuk withdrew from the District Council, leaving it without a quorum. There was an impasse. I remember hearing a rumour that Ejoku had sacrificed a black bull to ensure the success of his faction. A commission of enquiry was set up, and it reported in April 1958. It found Ejoku the main instigator of the problem. The Iseera promptly boycotted the District Council. In May the Governor visited, saw Ejoku and told him that he would have to go. So Ejoku retired. The council then accepted the reality of the situation: that Teso would revert to direct rule if they did not settle down. This affair was dealt with at senior level, but for a junior ADC was of considerable interest. It did not affect the day-to-day administration of the district. Touring continued and chiefs just got on with their jobs.

In January 1958 our second son, Nicholas, mostly known as Nick, was born in the Nakasero Hospital in Kampala. It was the height of the dry season. Following a scare when a wife from an up-country station had delayed going to Kampala and experienced a premature and difficult birth, it was decreed that the wives of European officials must go to Kampala a fortnight before the expected date of the birth. So Susan went to stay with her brother and his family in Kisubi. As was usual with her, Nick did not come early. In fact, she had a long and difficult labour, for much of which she was on her own in the labour ward. Susan was at this time very slim, having lost a great deal of weight in Soroti. Nick's first year of life was not an easy one for Susan or him. She was the first European mother in living memory to leave Nakasero Hospital breastfeeding.

During the Governor's visit in May, a light was thrown on Lady Crawford's character. Sir Frederick opened a new wing of the CMS hospital in Ngora. Lady Crawford came with him, though she loathed safari and grumbled constantly. She said she might have to return to Entebbe, as nanny was ill. Poor nanny was most upset by their absence. So Rosemary Griffith rang Government House. The governor's ADC said nanny was well and had gone to Kampala for lunch. Rosemary wrote a letter to Lady Crawford relaying this response. I had to take it thirty miles to Ngora.

Lady Crawford did not get on well with Lady Hartwell, the wife of the chief secretary. They could barely talk to each other. We were told of an amusing but unfortunate consequence. During a visit by the Queen Mother, the Crawfords gave a reception and dinner. Both ladies had each bought a very expensive dress, one from Nairobi and one from London. When the Hartwells arrived before the reception, the wives confronted each other in identical red dresses (it was said that there was only one other in the world). As there was no time for Lady Hartwell to return home and change, Lady Crawford had to rush upstairs and put on another dress.

There was a constant stream of visitors. A few stand out. One was Lady Barnett of the London County Council. An instruction had come from the Governor that she was to be put to no expense on her way to and from Karamoja. On her return journey, Susan and I were instructed to give her dinner, as we were the only admin couple in Soroti at that moment. Another ADC, I think Edward Cunningham, who had a well-developed sense of humour, attended. She was enthusiastic about Karamoja and 'the fine bodies' of the men. They only wore a piece of cloth tied at the shoulder, allowing most of them to be seen. The image of Lady Barnett admiring almost naked Karamojong had a certain charm. Another visitor who turned up without warning was a field officer (what in I cannot remember) who claimed to have been to King's, Canterbury, with me. He had been but I did not remember him. He was very large, and when he moved into the spare room he took dumb-bells and a mass of tinned food. We had no idea how long he would stay but, to our relief, it was only for a few days.

In July we went on local leave. We stayed first with Susan's brother, Peter, and his family. He was teaching at the Catholic College at Kisubi. From there we went to Kenya. The Kaptagat Arms was a haven for people from Eastern province. It was high, cool and needed log fires at night. On one visit there we heard two Kenya settler ladies discussing another guest, a doctor from Soroti. The settlers' dislike of government was well known. They thought him most charming 'even though he is government'. Then it was on to Nairobi, to stay with friends of my parents, the Sinclairs. Like the Boyds they had settled in Kenya between the wars. It was the slump and they nursed their coffee farm at Kibati, eating the same food as their workers. During and after the Second World War it prospered, and they had now handed it on to their sons and lived in a house on the Kibati road. They were most welcoming and agreed to look after the boys so we could go out one evening. They were not great baby-sitters, as we returned to find Adrian hysterical, believing himself abandoned. We then moved to stay again with the Boyds in Limuru. At that time it was still a bastion of the settler way of life. We saw a meet of the Limuru Hunt. Throughout this leave Nick was very unwell. He insisted on being breastfed and Susan, herself not well, had little milk. On return to Soroti I went straight out on safari.

The election of 1958 was a step towards self-government. Until then the Legislative Council had consisted of thirty-two official members and thirty representative members (eighteen African, six European and six Asian). The Legislative Council (Elections) Ordinance, passed in early October 1957, provided for the representative members to be elected. Previously, most of the eighteen representative members outside Buganda were nominated by the district councils and appointed by the Governor, who had in

Checking voting application forms with the chiefs

all cases accepted the nominations. The exceptions in the districts were Karamoja, which was represented by a backbench member (i.e. a member of the official side), and Bukedi, which refused to participate in the process. In Buganda the Electoral College made nominations. There would be no other changes to the constitution of the Legislative Council. This was in line with the statement of Her

Swearing in polling staff

Limuru Hunt

Majesty's Government when constitutional changes were introduced in mid-1955, that there would be no major changes to the constitution of Uganda until 1961. For the 1958 election Teso would form one electoral district.

The process began with the issue of election circulars on 18 December 1957 and 13 January 1958 by the supervisor of elections, C. P. S. (Peter) Allen. In Teso Edward Cunningham was made responsible, under the DC, for organising the election. When Edward was transferred to Jinja at the end of April, Arthur Watson took over. As a junior ADC I was told to supervise the registration of voters in Usuku county. This involved visiting the etem headquarters and examining the registration sheets, which were then taken to Soroti for inclusion in the preliminary registers. These were typed by clerks after they had been checked by a group of European wives to ensure they were completed correctly and the names deciphered, which was sometimes a real problem.

The Iteso took to the electoral process early; a system of elections to local councils was introduced in Teso in the late 1930s by the then DC,

F. R. Kennedy. For this election they registered in enormous numbers. The estimated electorate was 120,000. I do not have the final figure but, according to Edward, at the end of registration on 30 April, 152,000 Iteso had registered.

Preliminary registers were distributed on 21 June and a claims (for inclusion in the register) and objections (that someone was included twice or was not eligible) period ran from 25 June to 9 July. The job of ADCs was to tour each ebuku to see that the process was being carried out correctly. On 10 July we collected the claims and objection books from the ebuku headquarters.

The eitela was the polling division, so polling stations had to be found and prepared for the election. Many were in schools. Then polling staff had to be selected and trained. The training courses run by ADCs aimed to make sure the staff knew where they would work and the procedure for processing voters. Staff were then sworn in. As polling day approached I spent every day out visiting polling stations and training polling staff.

There were four candidates: three teachers and a businessman. Each had a symbol. Jehoshaphat Anyoti had an aeroplane; Raymond Imalingat a car; Cuthbert Obwangor a spear; and Daniel Odeke a lamp. They made use of their symbols. The aeroplane was very modern; the spear was a sign of strength.

Voting took place over three days: 20, 22 and 24 October. Ballot boxes, sealing pliers, voting stamps and registers had to be distributed on 16 and 17 October; I went to Kumi and Bukedea. On the three polling days I supervised stations in ibukui Soroti, Kumi and Amuria. Protectorate police were posted to polling stations with over 1,000 voters, but my recollection is of a smooth process without trouble. There were the usual incidents, such as an old lady who spent a long time in the booth trying to put her ballot paper into the keyhole of the ballot box. There were also demands from within the booths for the name of the person for whom to vote. Overall, in terms of procedure the election was a success. The local arrangements, which involved the presence of the eitela and erony (village) chiefs, and the apolon ateker (clan leaders) who could identify the voters, prevented fraud and double voting. Counting took place on 25 October (I was an enumerator) and Obwangor was elected.

TAX RIOT

1958 was also the year when graduated tax was introduced. It was intended to fund the growing operations of the District Council. The basic flaw of Poll Tax was that rich and poor paid the same. It could not be raised without penalising the poor. Graduated tax was a form of income and wealth tax. The basis on which assessments should be made was sent to chiefs. They were subject to checking. Some chiefs under-assessed and had to be instructed to reassess the householders. In ebuku Kumi, which had a young and energetic county chief, the assessments were tough. The result was trouble. The Eastern Province report for 1958, sent by the Provincial Commissioner, Tom Cox, states: 'There was an outbreak of violence at Kobwin (sub-county) where a crowd, resentful of the Graduated Tax assessments, got out of hand, attacked chiefs and burned records of the sub-county. Order was restored by Administrative Officers and a number of arrests were made by the Police. The machinery of appeal against assessment was overhauled to avoid the danger of a similar incident elsewhere.' Looking back, I realise that I had no apprehension that the people would attack us. Perhaps I had already absorbed the confidence of colonial administrators. In any case, the people expected to be able to complain to ADCs; so I was just fulfilling one of our basic functions.

A message arrived at the boma that rioting was taking place. Owen Griffith instructed me to go out and discover what was happening. Together with a clerk/interpreter I drove along the Mbale road and turned off on the road to Kobwin. A short way along we met the Sub-Inspector from Kumi police station with some of his constables. He strongly advised us not to go on. 'They have beaten us and will kill you.' With the confidence of youth I ignored his advice, and we drove on. At Kobwin the etem headquarters was surrounded by a crowd. We went in. The crowd filled the open hall while we stood on the platform at one end. Inevitably the crowd surged towards us, and the interpreter shouted that they were going to attack us. I did not think so and told the crowd to sit, which they immediately did. I then asked them to explain what was happening. A self-appointed spokesman complained about the assessments and the way they had been treated by the chiefs. I listened to others and it was clear to me that the crowd might have a point. The eitela chiefs were prudently absent but the sub-county chief gave his version. It seemed to me that the situation needed further examination, so I told the crowd that I had understood their complaints and would report to the DC. This satisfied the crowd, which by then was in a much better humour. I returned to Soroti and told the DC that I thought the people had a point. Owen arranged for another more experienced ADC, I think Arthur Watson, to carry out the review. The result was a reassessment accepted by the local people. The arrests must have taken place later.

The end of 1958 was grim for the children's health. The problems began with Adrian's hookworm. The treatment involved starving for twenty-four hours. At one point Adrian was so hungry that he asked to go into the kitchen. Susan reminded him that he could not have anything to eat. Adrian said he knew but would just like to look. The next day started with a purge, followed a couple of hours later by the worm medicine, a very bitter and burning fluid. Adrian took the medicine with a few tears. After another two hours he was given another purge and Susan promised him the treatment was over. Unfortunately, he could not eat until he had performed, and when the district medical officer called still nothing had happened. When we told the DMO, a good administrator without much human touch, he was determined that the dose should be repeated. Having promised Adrian that the treatment was over, Susan refused to do it. Exasperated, the DMO took the bottle and, saying the medicine was easy to administer, pinched Adrian's nose with one hand and tried to pour the medicine down his throat with the other hand. Adrian bit his finger; the doctor swore. The treatment failed, and we rejected a suggestion to try again in a couple of months. We had been told by a nurse that a new treatment powder was becoming available so we decided to wait until we went to the UK on leave. On leave in 1959 we obtained the new powder and empty capsules and filled them with the powder. After starving Adrian took around twenty capsules. Being almost four he accepted the need for treatment. It worked.

In November Nick had a bad tummy. The same doctor said that it was a secondary infection from his ears. Susan knew it was really a tummy bug but the doctor refused to accept it. Nick continued to have a runny tummy for a few days. One evening he clearly began to deteriorate. Susan pushed him round in his pram all night. As he got dehydrated he moaned constantly. Susan's mother walked with her, wringing her hands, saying that 'little children just die in the tropics'. At 7 o'clock Susan sent our houseboy to the doctor, saying that she needed him to come urgently. He was the sort of doctor who did not respond to 'fussing mothers,' so he did not come until 8.30. When he saw Nick he said he had to go straight to Mbale and be put on a drip. I was, inevitably, on safari, so the newly arrived ADC, Ken Scott, was told by the DC to take Susan and Nick to Mbale. The doctor in Mbale was warned.

At the Mbale hospital Nick was desperate for water, but the Nursing Sister refused on the grounds that they had to wait for the doctor. By then Nick was being sick and pointing to the water jugs and was obviously not far from death. The Provincial Medical Officer arrived after 1 o'clock. Of course Nick could have water. He confirmed what Susan had suspected: Nick had gastroenteritis. At 2 o'clock Nick was given ambramycin, a raspberry-coloured anti-biotic which had just arrived in Uganda. It was to be 'treated like gold dust'. The effect was immediate. Susan described it as being like a flower opening in a Walt Disney film. It undoubtedly saved his life. A message reached me on safari and I drove down that evening with Adrian and Susan's mother. We stayed for three days at the Barbers' and were then able to take Nick back to Soroti. The memory of this episode still distresses me.

Nick did not really get over his illness until we went on UK leave. During the leave he and Adrian spent a month with my parents on Alderney while we went on holiday to France and Italy. It was lovely for my parents, who got to know their grandchildren. My mother gave them her good plain cooking and insisted that Nick rested, which he did, sleeping for hours every afternoon. When we met them at Gatwick they had red cheeks and energy. At St Benedict's School Nick had a TB vaccination, which reacted, but nothing was done to follow this up. Later still, when Nick was training to be a doctor, he underwent a medical examination. The X-ray showed old TB lesions, probably another legacy of Soroti.

Adrian was the next victim. On a Sunday at the end of November, Susan and I went to Mass. When we returned home we found Adrian lying on our bed screaming. He said that he did not want dawa (medicine). We said there was no need for him to worry about having dawa. Ludya said that during the normal morning walk, with Nick in the pram and Adrian walking, he suddenly announced that he could not walk. She put him in the pram with Nick and brought him home. We could not persuade Adrian to try to walk. So we called the doctor, who, this time, came at once. He could not find anything wrong and Adrian, under strong pressure, staggered a few steps. It was not polio.

On Monday I set out to complete my safari. Adrian would not go to sleep at all and wanted to be constantly entertained. He talked all through the night and wanted to move from bed to bed. This performance was repeated the next night. Susan got desperate and called the doctor again. He said he would give Adrian an injection which would put him out for twenty-four hours. He would call back during the evening. Within twenty minutes Adrian was awake. When the doctor returned, he swore (again). He began to talk of sending Adrian to Kampala on his own. The implication was that Susan was unable to cope with him; she was not firm enough. Later Adrian began to sweat, not just a gentle perspiration but flooding. Susan cut his hair to cool him, during which he went to sleep. At the end of the week I returned from safari and Adrian staggered down the front steps to greet me, the first steps he had taken since the previous Sunday. He quickly recovered, almost the next day, and was able to go in a Swiss Guard uniform, made by Susan's mother, to the children's Christmas party, where he won first prize.

So what was it? It may have been a fever, unknown, which broke with the sweating. Keith Batten's opinion was that Adrian had taken a local stimulant, probably when he was with Ludya in the servants' quarters. Ludya certainly clammed up after the initial account she gave. Moreover, we knew she was desperate to have a child and might have been taking a stimulant. Also, why should Adrian complain about 'dawa'?

The doctor continued to believe that Adrian's attack was psychological so in January we went to see the consultant in Kampala. He also did not know the cause of the attack but thought that it might be his relationship with Susan's mother. By this time she had left Soroti, and I had to write and tell her the consultant's opinion, which in essence was that she had to show Adrian great affection no matter how he behaved. She did not like the implied criticism. Adrian had not met any other old person and she assumed he would automatically love her as 'family'. Later, after Uganda, they had a very good friendship.

The Christmas of 1958 was full of the usual parties for adults and children. The swimming pool outside the club was in full operation. Susan's mother had put her great skill at sewing fancy dresses to full use, not only the Swiss Guard uniform for Adrian but also created Perseus and Medusa costumes for us. The snakes in Susan's hair were pieces of bark cloth with eyes and mouth painted on them. Wires attached them to Susan's hair. We won!

The European cemetery lay below Soroti Rock near the PWD yard. The township labour made sure it was kept in good order. When Susan and I returned in 1996 it was overgrown and some of the headstones had fallen. The labour also dug the graves on the rare occasions when they were needed. It was hard work cutting through the murram. It happened twice during our time in Soroti. On the first occasion a visitor in the Soroti rest house died. The second was the manager of the Swedish drilling firm which had the contract for drilling boreholes in the district. It was an important programme, as it brought more easily accessible water to the people and their livestock in the drier parts of the district. The manager was 'Pop' Neilsen, who lived with his wife, Anna, in Soroti. Anna was famous for her aphorism 'Life is 'ell in zee tropics'. They were much liked. Anna died on their leave, during which their houseboy, Opolot, had come to us asking for temporary work, which we gave him. He left us when 'Pop' returned on his own. In February 1959 'Pop' died of a heart attack in the dry season, when the weather was extremely hot. The law required that he be buried within a day.

I had just had a bout of tummy trouble but was able to supervise the preparations. There was usually a grave dug ready but it was decided that it was too close to the hedge which ran around the cemetery. So the township labour toiled at digging a new grave, periodically visited by me. The wives collected such flowers they could find, mostly bougainvillea, for laying on the coffin. When Susan took her offering round to the house she found Opolot wandering sadly about, not knowing what to do. She took him to the funeral.

'Pop' was not a practising Christian but a priest would hold a service at the graveside. Normally burials took place early in the morning, but the plane from Nairobi bringing his senior colleagues did not arrive until after 11 o'clock. The funeral did not take place until noon, when the heat was tremendous. The coffin was brought on a trailer drawn by a tractor. It was then carried to the grave by a team of European colleagues from the station, one of whom stumbled and almost collapsed under its weight. It was placed over the grave. It was immediately apparent that it would not fit. The sweating labour worked at the hole as we waited in the boiling sun. The flowers drooped. Eventually the service, a shortened version, was held and the coffin lowered into the grave, where it rested at an angle. When the congregation left the labourers raised the coffin, enlarged the hole, and 'Pop' was properly buried. All seemed well.

Adrian, Christmas 1958

After the funeral his colleagues went through 'Pop's' papers and found one stating that he did not wish a Christian burial but to be cremated and his ashes joined with Anna's in Sweden. There was acceptance that we should try to meet his wishes. The problem was

Perseus and Medusa. The Roman is Paddy Foley –
his helmet an inverted cake stand

The winner

that the law required permission from Entebbe for a body to be dug up. Owen Griffith rang Tom Cox, the PC, who said that the coffin should be removed immediately and quietly. Arrangements were made with the Hindu community for 'Pop' to be cremated at their ghat. I told the astonished and exhausted labour to dig him up. Everyone involved was sworn to silence about this breach of the law. Under the eyes of the Nairobi representatives, the coffin was loaded onto a pick-up truck and taken to the ghat. After the evening meeting of the ayahs and their charges, Ludya came back agog to tell us that 'Pop' had been dug up and burnt. So much for station secrecy.

Soroti fell into the Mill Hill Fathers' diocese of Tororo. Their local parish was based on the mission at Madera, outside Soroti. There was also a convent of the Sisters of St Francis, in whose chapel I was received into the Catholic Church. So Madera had the parish church but a Mill Hill Father came each Sunday to the Goan Institute to say Mass. The parish priest was Father Straeter, an eccentric Dutchman with a passion for tennis. He insisted on playing in the Soroti Club tournament, which took place over the Easter weekend, when we expected him to be devoting himself to the services in Madera. An example of his quirky character was his attempt to tame a python bought for 5 Shs. He brought it to tennis and tried to induce it to leave its box so that we could admire it. His attempts produced hisses, and the python tried to bite anyone getting close. Father Straeter was a little put out and we never heard the fate of the snake. I hope it was released. After our return to the UK we exchanged letters with Father Straeter, but, as often happens, the letters stopped and we do not know what happened to him.

Our particular friend among the Mill Hill Fathers was Louis Albers, another Dutchman, who was the Catholic chaplain at Teso College. He was a priest with a deep understanding of human problems and a willingness to bend the rules if he thought it was for the good of the people consulting him. Altogether a very human and kind man, but not a softie. He told us that on the night before his ordination, when he was praying in the chapel, an old missionary priest, back on leave and unknown to Louis, tapped him on the shoulder and offered him prayers and advice. He said that Louis could go through his priestly life with all his emotions intact, living on a knife edge but open and responsive to the problems of others; or he could shut down every emotion, which would be easier for him but of no use to anyone else. There were plenty of examples of the latter approach.

Towards the end of 1958 Susan's health was not good and her weight had fallen to nearly 7 stone. Louis reacted in two ways. He told her that she should not have another child until her health was better and indicated that she should accept the use of contraception. Remember that this was long before Vatican II. The Catholic Church stressed that only the 'safe period' (a misnomer for many people) might be used. His other response was to cook us marvellous meals. One which he cooked, and brought to our house, was a four-course 'Diner de Consolation' for which I still have the menu. He also introduced her to gin and cinzano, still a favourite tipple.

We kept in touch with Louis after we left Uganda. He would send us copies of notes of his courses explaining Vatican II and occasionally came to see us. His sister came to stay with us in London before her marriage. In the late 1960s he had a stroke and was sent by his order to Canada, where he died.

The only other Mill Hill Father we got to know was Father Galvin, who gave me instruction before I was received into the Catholic Church. It consisted in plodding through the catechism question by question without any discussion, in a way suitable for small children. He also gave instruction to Ken Savage, a PWD officer married to a Polish Catholic, Teresa, who had also decided to become a Catholic. He was not a good teacher. When one went to Father Galvin for confession, every sin confessed was attributed to the climate.

In 1959, after the election, the work of ADCs resumed its usual pattern of touring, and, like others, we put up visitors and those needing a base when they were about to go on leave or on a posting to another district. In a letter of early February, Susan listed recent activities: 'The end of last week was all safari. I enjoyed it very much but Adrian got rather bored. And this week is mine for taking the children to and from school which seems to leave little time in between. Now tomorrow night I have the Bleaches and the new Police people coming to dinner. We have to put someone up from Moroto on Saturday night and the poor Trathens [agricultural officer] who go to Mbale on Monday after spending Sunday night here. We also had strange people to lunch yesterday so life has been rather full.' Another letter in April continued the same theme.

It was the height of the dry season in February. Salatieri thought the rains were close. That did not help when the Provincial Commissioner visited. He liked everyone in ties and jackets even though the temperature was in the 90s Fahrenheit. So we sweltered until he left.

One of my few diary entries was for 27 February, Adrian's birthday. It shows the range of jobs carried out by ADCs.

> Rain in the afternoon when Phil Reed [the health officer] and I went counting ice creams that will be destroyed. The analyst's report showed that they contained germs of food poisoning, scarlet fever and other diseases. The reaction of the Indian shop owners was 'what will happen to our trade? Don't you worry, we will be able to sell them.' However all the deep freezes are sealed and we await the result of tests at the Kampala factory.

In April Hugh Salmon, a young ADC, married Helena in Soroti. It was a formal affair for Soroti, with a wedding cake sent from Nairobi. The weather was not really hot but Susan and most other wives removed their stockings before joining the reception. However, a young wife, not married that long herself, put on her going away clothes, suitable for March in the UK, and fainted. Wives gathered round to loosen her clothes, including her corsets, stockings, etc.

There has been much written about the pecking order in colonial countries and the deference due to senior officers and their wives. According to stories we heard, seniority and precedence were important in the past. In our time I found very little of this in Uganda, though there was an understood pecking order. In an up-country station it was accepted, because it was obvious, that the DC was the senior official in the district. It was true that as Administrative Officers we automatically had status, and this was sometimes resented. Even as junior Administrative Officers we would receive invitations which would not go to junior officers in other departments. Generally, everyone mixed easily. Occasionally wives asserted for themselves their husband's status. When we first arrived the DC's wife told Susan occasionally who should be invited to dinner or came to see why we had not been to a club event. We were reminded to 'play our part on the station'. I think this was a way of showing young ADCs their responsibilities. In Mbarara the DC, Hugh Fraser, was not at that time married and was not a person who worried about status. Moreover, we were by then more senior.

In May Susan and the children flew to the UK a few weeks before my six months' leave was due to start. Much of my time was then spent on safari. In June I spent twenty-one days on safari in ebuku Kaberamaido and ebuku Amuria. In July I ran law courses for etem chiefs and court clerks. The main objective was to explain the approach to be taken in civil and criminal cases, which inevitably overlapped.

I enjoyed the visits to ebuku Amuria most. One, on 25 June, was with Mr Andriades, the Teso District Council's head of works, to site a hospital and maternity unit in Kapelabyong, a new etem. There was also a new smart rest house where I stayed. It stood on a ridge looking across open country to the Labwor Hills. The front room was open providing an all-round view. The rest house was on a path to the Roman Catholic primary school. The less brave children would run across the compound giggling while the bold either sauntered across staring at me or came up and greeted me, much my preferred response.

I was not visiting ebuku Usuku so much as there had been no cattle theft by the Karamajong so far in 1959. The only incident was caused by Iteso raiding and killing a number of cattle. The government response was firm, and some twenty-five people were imprisoned and ordered to pay 140 head of cattle. In 1996, when we returned to Teso, there were very few cattle to be seen. The Karamojong had been armed and let loose on Teso. They removed all the cattle.

The only other excitement was the rumour of a strike by servants for higher wages. Some more aggressive wives were up in arms and called meetings of wives and bachelors. As we paid Salatieri above the going rate, I doubted if he would strike. Nothing came of all the fuss.

CLIMBING NAPAK

Towards the end of June Ken Scott, another ADC, and I climbed Napak, one peak of an extinct volcano just over the Karamoja border. We were to have been joined by Sam Osmont, a Shell rep. Sam's attractive wife, Lolly, could not come as she became breathless on even a small climb. In the event Sam had to cry off, as he was inflicted with a visit from a senior Shell sales manager. The arrangements were uncertain; we had no idea if we had taken the right kit. We were warned that the Topeth who lived on the top of Napak expected one to act as a doctor. One climber had been presented with a bare bottom with a sore on it.

We left late Friday afternoon and arrived at Iriri after dark, to discover that the chief who was expected to make the arrangements for the climb was ill. So we went to the house of the stockman, Pat Curtis (there was a large cattle quarantine compound and market near the Teso–Karamoja border), reaching it after many wrong turnings on the maze of tracks. He was, fortunately, at home, a pair of extended Uniport huts. He gave us beds and a meal and undertook to find us porters and a guide for the next day. Unsurprisingly, his house was visited by animals; a leopard was a regular visitor, and that night the hyenas howled within fifty yards of the house. Ever since my childhood in Nairobi, when I would listen to the sound of hyenas, their howls *are* Africa for me. Pat left early to get meat for the porters but drove into an anthill, putting his Land-Rover out of action. We did not see him again that day.

We left Iriri at about nine o'clock, and after taking our Land-Rover for about an hour and a half reached a path up the mountain. We allocated the loads to the porters. The first part of the climb up a valley was hard work, mainly because it was airless and steamy. The porters expected frequent stops and after an hour and a half climb came to a homestead with a muddy compound and no view. We refused to stop, to the dismay of the porters, and went on until at about one o'clock we reached a ridge near another homestead. After lunch we rested during the afternoon. About six o'clock it began to rain. The porters, a Native Government askari and our district administration driver were miserable, so we gave them the outer fly of our tent. The rain poured down and it was obvious that the outer and inner flies of the tent were by themselves inadequate protection. The porters and the others went into the nearby home and Ken and I tried to stick it out. When it became obvious that the beds and clothes would be soaked we put them under the groundsheet on which we perched. After an hour and a half the rain stopped, the sky cleared and we changed our clothes and prepared our supper. We then sat drinking beer by the fire lit by the porters. Sleep came quickly, but about one o'clock the rain began again, but luckily not hard. There was nothing we could do so we pulled the blankets over our heads and went to sleep. At dawn we had breakfast and after breaking camp sent the porters down to our Land-Rover.

We were fortunate in our guide. The day before we had met a group of Topeth, one of whom hid his spear and joined us. He had shown us the night's campsite and the next day returned to show us the way to the top. He was a delightful person, courteous throughout; a contrast to the porters, who were pleasant rogues. We left for the top at 8.40 and arrived after a hard two-hour climb. Just below the top was a glen with a clear stream flowing off the cliff face. Nearby were some beautifully shaped trees, a contrast to the bush trees on the way up. The last part of the climb was over moorland with wild hyacinths. As we arrived the cloud was beginning to form on the crater face, rising out of nothing, like steam. The weather was too hazy for the best views but we had been able to see the Suk Hills from our camp. The summit was next to the crater edge, with a straight fall of thousands of feet. After an hour and a half at the top, when the cloud was getting thicker, we started our descent. Within a quarter of a mile it was drizzling and soon the rain came. For over half the way down it poured. Our clothes were soon soaked, but my only concern was for the film in my camera. As soon as the rain stopped we quickly dried and continued to descend at a great rate, taking just under two hours to get to the Land-Rover. The road from Nabilatuk to Iriri was a mess after the rain of the previous night and we stuck in the mud a couple of times. The black cotton soil was so disgusting that I took off my shoes to push the Land-Rover. After a couple of beers with Pat Curtis, which I regretted, we set out for Soroti. I slept well that night.

The pace of political development was increasing. On 17 November 1958, shortly after the general election, the Governor established a constitutional committee with John Wild as chairman. Its purpose was 'to consider and recommend the form of direct elections on a common roll... and the method of ensuring that there will be adequate representation on the Legislative Council for non-Africans'. The members consisted of ten Africans, two Asians and two Europeans. The secretary was Frank Kalimuzo. The committee toured Uganda, holding meetings to take evidence. In early July they visited Soroti. In a letter to Susan dated 5 July, I wrote:

> Frank arrived in good form and we got on well. He seems very happy with his wife who sounds a dear but can only speak a little English. She is expecting a baby in about five months. Frank is getting on well with his work and the experience of working with John Wild is excellent... The Committee themselves are pleasant and relaxed. There were the inevitable parties, one by the Secretary General [of Teso District Council] and another by Arthur [Watson, acting DC] and Mary. The African members of the Committee mixed easily. They [the committee] have heard the most utter rubbish everywhere

and though the African members obviously realise that the public is in general hopelessly ignorant about politics, I doubt if they can admit this publicly without injuring their political careers. Their questions were good. They clearly see many of the difficulties ahead and what is more, by their questions, make the people giving evidence aware of the difficulties. I think the District Council delegation expected to have their say and get out, but they were given a gruelling questioning which shattered them. The best evidence was given by a group of women from Madera. Incidentally when the District Council was going to give evidence Arthur made a move to leave but was immediately asked to stay to give them moral support.

Loading the porters on Napak

Porters resting on Napak

When the committee reported, its main recommendations were that there should be elections on a common roll of voters over eighteen but no special arrangements for non-Africans and no safeguards for Buganda.

Susan and I thought it would be a good idea to thank Salatieri for all his work by giving him a calf. In mid-July Fin Haddock, the District Veterinary Officer, took Salatieri and me to the cattle auction in Arapai, just outside Soroti. We left the choice of calf to Salatieri, and he bought a bull calf which looked in good shape. I asked the calf's name. He smiled and said 'Amusugun' – i.e. European.

Towards the end of our tour there was growing pressure for an increase in the salaries of civil servants in Uganda. The Uganda European Civil Servants Association submitted a claim to the Uganda government on 15 May 1959. The association held meetings around Uganda, one in Soroti. There was talk of officials resigning if an increase was not agreed. It was hard to say how real this threat actually was. The award of an increase of £200 p.a. to Permanent Secretaries, all Administrative Officers, increased the irritation of officers in technical departments about the 'admin'.

After a year without a response from the Uganda government, the Association considered that there was nothing to be gained by waiting for their reply and submitted a claim direct to London. A letter was sent to Harold Macmillan in 10 Downing Street, bypassing Ian McLeod, the Secretary of State. Direct claims had also been submitted from Kenya, Tanganyika, Nigeria and Nyasaland. In July 1960 the Fleming Salaries Commission arrived in Uganda. A group of Administrative Officers in Entebbe and Kampala set up an informal group to represent Administrative Officers throughout Uganda in discussions with the commission. Professional and technical officers already had their own association.

The commission toured Uganda, holding meetings, and were given a tough time. The problem in all the east African territories was the delay in increasing pay. The situation was not improved when, in November 1960, the Economy Commission recommended that there should be no interim award, and stated that the provincial administration was overstaffed and that mileage allowances were too high and should be reduced. Many officials survived on their mileage allowance. By February 1961 there was still no agreement. Eventually salaries were increased; mine in May 1962 was £1,491 p.a. At the end of my final leave in October 1962 it was £1,554 p.a. A letter of 9 May 1961 from the Colonial Office to the Treasury stated: 'The information we are getting from East Africa suggests that the effects of the Fleming salaries coupled with the White Paper Scheme [on compensation for early retirement] has resulted in considerable improvement in morale.'

All staff going to the UK on leave were required to have a medical examination in case there was any condition which should be treated in the UK. At the end of July I was told that I had a positive Widal test, indicating paratyphoid. I was told to report to the Tropical Diseases Hospital in London. After tests the consultant told me that all were negative and that I was 'the victim of upcountry medicine'. Towards the end of the tour, I found myself increasingly tired. One tour, in ebuku Serere, had to be cut short as I could not work properly. The cause was not clear but I suspect it was what was called 'suppressed malaria'. The Paludrine pills prevented full-scale malaria but the infection left one tired and low.

THOUGHTS AT THE END OF THE TOUR

This first tour was tough for Susan and the boys. Soroti was not a healthy posting but, looking back, I still remember it in many ways as a time of interesting and enjoyable moments. In particular, Soroti was a friendly place, and we made friends with whom we are still in touch. Despite Susan's reservations early in the tour, the way of life suited us; it was a good mixture of work and play.

I can see that I was lucky in my colleagues. Owen Griffith, who had been Cohen's private secretary before becoming DC Teso, had been tolerant, and, after the brief introduction to the role of an Administrative Officer, had let me get on with the duties assigned to me. He guided me through my first safari and then let me out on my own. Responsibility for the township of Soroti was easily monitored, as failure would have been obvious. The system of 'flimsies', a file containing copies of letters (except confidential and sensitive correspondence from the DC) which was circulated round the administrative officers, enabled him to keep an eye on what his juniors were doing. This approach to new Administrative Officers meant that I had to grow up quickly. It was a way of sorting the competent and incompetent. While some basic training is necessary, the modern system of seemingly endless courses has gone too far the other way.

Owen's first priorities were the political and economic development of Teso, and the maintenance of law and order. In this work he was the leader of the district team, which produced and implemented the district plan. In their day-to-day work the Administrative Officers, as often as not, consulted the senior ADC, in our case Arthur Watson, rather than the DC. In Teso the DC and ADC1 were a team, an arrangement reinforced by their marriage to sisters.

What was obvious by the middle of 1959 was that self-government was imminent. The younger Administrative Officers I met all believed that independence would not be long delayed. Nevertheless, it never occurred to me not to return at the end of leave. We had no idea that independence would come as soon as it did.

The administrative system at district level, as I saw it in Teso, worked well. Thanks to the close working relationship between the Protectorate Government and District Council officials, particularly the ebuku and etem chiefs, there was stability. The education system and the economy were improving; law and order prevailed in general. Even tribal fighting was under control. There was a system for dealing with complaints through the meetings held on safari. Administrative Officers were ombudsmen of a kind. It was less clear how such a system could be modified to allow greater democratic control of government without lowering administrative standards.

Chapter 8

Long Leave

On 22 July my 'effects' were taken for storage in Kampala, and I flew to the UK on 25 July. It was good to be reunited with my family. Six months' leave sounds marvellous. Some of it was. After staying in Alderney with my parents, I attended a town and country planning summer school in Buckingham. It took me into a quite different part of government, which was one of its attractions.

The problem of long leave, unless one had a house as base, was the need to stay either in a hotel or lodgings, or with family and friends. The children found this style of living most unsatisfactory. Their only long stay was with my parents in Alderney, when Susan, her sister Barbara and I went for a month to France and Italy in September and early October.

This trip was the highlight of the leave. We began by going to Paris to collect our new Citroën ID19 from the factory on the outskirts of Paris. We then drove to Cluny for the night, staying at a pension run by a chef who had worked for Lyons in the Trocadero. He had a strong London accent. His brother had also worked for Lyons. As he said: 'My family have always worked for Lyonses.' The food was delicious. I remember in particular his onion soup. The only drawback was the double bed, which had a steep camber on each side towards a ravine along the middle. We each had to cling to the edge of our side of the bed. Next stop Turin, where our car was bounced round by the hotel staff so that it could get into the hotel courtyard from a narrow cobbled street. Here I remember my introduction to delicious Italian antipasto.

The visit to Assisi was special. Both Susan and I have a great devotion to St Francis and were able to go to many of the places associated with him, the Carceri, the Gubbio and the Church of St Clare. There were not the crowds of tourists that now reduce the pleasure of such visits. We toured the Cathedral of San Francisco on a day of pouring rain. Our guidebook mentioned a museum of church chalices, crosses and vestments. We were unable to find it, but luck was with us. We came upon a small group in dripping mackintoshes being given a tour by a very smooth English Franciscan. We stood on the fringe of the group and listened to the descriptions of parts of the cathedral. The Franciscan clearly did not like our presence. He then referred to the museum. This was our opportunity, and we were delighted when the Franciscan unlocked a massive door and guided the group, including ourselves, into the museum. He then made clear the reason for his dislike of our presence by saying loudly 'If you would come this way, Your Majesty'; 'I think you will find this crucifix interesting, Your Majesty'. We were a bit shaken but the door was locked. We identified an obvious protection officer and explained our problem. He was entirely relaxed and advised us to look around. So we went ahead, amazed at the collection of rich treasure kept by the Franciscans, who are meant to be an order of 'poor' friars. When we had seen enough, the protection officer had a word with a friar by the door and we escaped. The royals were the king and queen of Sweden (Louise Mountbatten, who was English).

Another highlight was a night's stay in Orvieto. Our room in the elderly hotel on the main square had a splendid painted ceiling. The weather was still warm so we had dinner at a table in the square. The cool Orvieto wine was another great memory. I still love this wine.

The weather stayed warm throughout our time in Italy. We would always have a picnic lunch. In early October our Italian money ran out and we went over the mountains to France, where the heavens opened and the temperature fell. We went back to Cluny for two nights, lured by the wonderful food and in spite of the bed. This time we did not even try to sleep in it and dossed down on the floor. Being at the end of our tour we could only afford breakfast and an evening meal. The pangs of hunger as dinner approached were terrible. We then drove into Paris, where disaster struck. I was looking for a street before turning left across the centre of one of Paris's squares, a starburst of streets. As I turned a young man on a scooter struck my bonnet and bounced off, breaking his leg. A woman in a shop shouted 'Assassin!'. Barbara, a nurse, took the rug from our car, placing it over the young man. An ambulance soon arrived with police, who told me to go to the nearby police station. There I rang the local insurance agent. The police wanted to take a statement but I declined until an English interpreter came. There was a long wait, spent reading. Eventually a helpful police interpreter arrived and I explained what had happened. He turned out to be a sergeant who had served with the British forces during the war. The insurance agent arrived and spoke to the police. He was very gloomy. However, after a short wait the police said that they were not going to pursue the matter and said we could leave. It was, however, too late to make our planned visit to Versailles. I heard later that the insurance company had paid compensation as I was at fault because I was making the turn. There followed a marvellous week of theatre visits and concerts in London. Then we went to Gatwick Airport to meet Adrian and Nicholas, who were escorted by my mother. Their obvious good health was a real pleasure.

At the end of my tour in Teso, the suggestion was made that I would be posted to Karamoja on my return from leave. In November Don Marshall, the Permanent Secretary at the Ministry of Local Government, wrote that I would be going to Ankole. Towards the end of the leave the prospect of returning to Uganda to a house of one's own was increasingly attractive. I flew to Entebbe on 18 January 1960 and reported for duty in Mbarara on 24 January. Susan and the children had stayed in the UK until after 20 January, when Nicholas had his second birthday and became entitled to a seat for himself on the plane.

Chapter 9

Ankole District

Our first house in Mbarara – No. 97 – was modern and of slightly eccentric design. There was a good sitting room but one of the bedrooms was on its own, up stairs direct from the sitting room. The garden was on a slope and without a view. I agitated for a move, and on 16 April we moved to House No. 1, an old-style house with a view over the town towards Masaka. We could see the Masaka road curving up the hills in the distance. No. 1 had good-sized rooms and a verandah front and rear. Later we persuaded the PWD to extend the guest bathroom at the back of the house to include a loo and put an expanded metal grille around the back verandah so the boys' toys could be kept there.

When Susan and I returned to Mbarara in 1996, No. 1 was the telephone exchange, replacing the one in the town which had been destroyed when the Tanzanian troops fought their way through the town. The house was in good condition and surrounded by a high fence. We walked through the front gate, went to a man who appeared to be in charge and told him why we were there. He was delighted and showed us over the building while we explained the function of each room during our time there; most, unsurprisingly, full of telephone equipment. We signed the visitors' book. On the way round a man, who turned out to be the general

House No. 1, Mbarara

handyman, came up to us and asked if we recognised him. I confessed I did not. He said we had two sons – true. He then said that he had delivered our milk, and I remembered the milkman on his bicycle with a small churn on the back carrier riding up to the kitchen door. It was thirty-four years since he had seen us.

Teso and Ankole were very different. It was partly the climate; Teso was hot and dry; Ankole, with its green countryside and high hills, cooler and infinitely more healthy. There was a fireplace in No. 1 which we occasionally used. That was not all. Teso, with its open country and wide skies, was a wilder Africa; Ankole, a kingdom with its Bahima aristocracy, had a more sophisticated feel. As people we preferred the Iteso, with their directness. Soroti and Mbarara as postings were also different. Both had supportive communities but Soroti's mixed better and was more friendly. It was more family-orientated. For ADCs there was another difference: Mbarara had an officer solely responsible for the town, so the junior ADC avoided that chore.

Susan liked Mbarara because she had more settled jobs and, for most of the time, was the only admin wife. She also enjoyed the very active drama group. The fact that we were better off and more

155

experienced made a considerable difference to our lives. Generally, District Officers preferred their first district to their later postings. I certainly did, despite the problems we had in Teso.

As in Soroti we began badly with servants. The cook we took on in January went in March, as we found him disagreeable, grumpy and surly. In March, while we were away at the Katunguru Regatta in the Kazinga channel between Lakes Edward and George, our house was burgled. The servants, John the houseboy and Miriam the ayah, who were meant to be guarding the house, obviously failed. So they went, and we persuaded Salatieri to come from Teso. He arrived in June, returning home to collect his wife, who stayed with us until September. It was such a relief. He brought with him, at our request, someone from his village to be houseboy. He was Thomas, the brother of William, our servant in Soroti.

When Salatieri went on holiday in March 1961 we took on temporarily Juma bin Saidi, who came from Tanganyika. He was a bit 'beautiful' and average in his skills. Not long after his arrival we had an argument over pay. At first he said he would leave, so we retrieved the back door key from him. A little later he changed his mind, and we restored the key to him, reminding him that his employment was temporary. He then disappeared and after three days I went to the police, to discover that he had been arrested wearing stolen trousers and shoes. A note was delivered to me from Juma in prison (on remand) authorising his brother, Abdulla bin Sef, to collect his belongings. By this time Juma had gone to court, and Maurice Phelan, the magistrate, cautioned him as it was his first recorded offence. As Juma had not returned we went into his quarters. They were very neat. A large mirror hung from the ceiling above the bed. There was a locked trunk, which I took to the police. As it had been at my house, the Chief Superintendent sought my agreement to forcing open the trunk. It was full of our things – table cloths, sheets and ornaments. Juma had an unfulfilled desire for decorative objects. In many ways he was a sad case.

We also had two temporary servants, both students. The first was Severo, recommended by Susan's brother, Adrian Hastings, then a priest in Masaka diocese. He was said to want to be a priest but we did not detect much of a vocation in him. Severo lived in our servants' quarters during his holidays and did a variety of tasks. He was totally without go or initiative. The other was Lawrence, a student working for his Higher Certificate who lived locally. He was completely different, having plenty of go. He worked in the garden, but without any knowledge of flowers. We had to give him careful instructions. Unfortunately, this did not always work. The Community Development Officer and his wife were very keen gardeners and grew flowers that most of us could not. Their pride and joy were double-ruffled petunias. They asked us to cherish them when they went on leave, so they were moved into a bed in the front of our house. We explained to Lawrence how delicate and special they were. He then 'weeded' them and we had the uncomfortable job of explaining what had happened.

After the burglary we acquired a large dog, a labrasatian, with yellow eyes like a lion and a thick black mane. He looked terrifying but was in reality soft. The boys were asked to give him a name. Their first offering was Lionstein! Where they found such a name was unclear. We rejected it. They then suggested Lacey, which stuck. He was a good guard dog. One of the traditional routes to the town below passed through our garden, and more than once he chased people walking along this route. One of them had to climb a tree, where he stayed until we rescued him. He claimed later to the police that he was taking the direct route from his village to the town. Another of Lacey's contributions to our safety was the discovery of a snake in our wood store near the kitchen door. The servants agreed that a snake had gone in. They removed the wood carefully and eventually found the snake, a sand viper. I dispatched it with a golf club. The only other result of this incident was that my legs were covered with the fleas that infested the store.

Lacey loved chasing the golf totos (children) who caddied on the course across the road from our garden. He liked nipping their ankles. We tried to break him of this pleasure but without much success. His one, serious, drawback was that he was not house-trained, despite our best efforts. So at night he was tied to the railings of the verandah with enough rope to get into the front garden to relieve himself. This arrangement did not always work, as he relieved himself on the verandah, and on a couple of occasions climbed through the verandah railings and fell into the canna bed below.

Our servants shared Lacey's robust attitude to anyone entering our property. On one occasion we were being visited by my brother-in-law, Adrian. One evening he looked into the garden and saw a man rummaging in his car. I rushed out. The man fled, but I caught him, because he fell over the edge of one of the small terraces which ran across the lawn. He was submissive, but the servants, who had quickly appeared, collected their spears and stood guard over him until the police arrived. I heard later that he was recently out of prison. He was sent back for another year.

When we left, in 1962, we were most concerned about Lacey's future. I offered him to a fellow ADC, Emmanuel Wakhweya, later to become Finance Minister under Amin before going into exile. Emmanuel agreed to have Lacey and the last we saw of him was seated on the back seat of Emmanuel's car, obviously very pleased with himself.

Back to 1960. Just below our garden was the DC's house. Hugh had a devoted but slightly deranged Dalmatian called Humphrey. Occasionally we looked after Humphrey. On one occasion he was so disturbed by Hugh's departure on a journey that he followed the car for at least five miles along the Masaka road. He was eventually brought to us, with the pads of his paws raw. We put on ointment and tied socks over the paws, which he, of course, tried to remove.

As in Soroti, the centre of the European community's social life was the club. Golf was an important element, though not for me, and the climate made it possible to keep the course more like the courses in Kenya. There were also two tennis courts. We played cricket matches, and on one occasion a rugger game, against a visiting Entebbe team. I played scrum half, my position at school, and regretted it as my legs were grazed and bruised by the hard ground.

The entrance to the club led to the bar, with a long counter, and a room to the right was large enough for dances, such as those on St Andrew's night and New Year. When Susan and I visited Mbarara in 1996 the club looked unchanged. The shields listing the golf captains were in place, with the names just changing from European to Ugandan. A board was up showing the result of the previous weekend's golf competition. A course was being run in the events room and a man, the Regional Veterinary Officer, greeted us, introducing himself as the club chairman. He invited us to the 'guest night' that evening, which with much regret we had to decline as we were booked into Mweya Lodge in the Queen Elizabeth National Park. The feeling of the club was virtually unchanged.

Towards the end of our tour, when independence was in sight, there was a debate in the club about admitting people of all races as members. To us in the Administration, there could be no question of not changing. There were, however, some members in other departments who saw no need for variation of the rules of membership; they did not appear to realise that the approach of independence required any adjustments. Fortunately, the change was agreed when the matter was put to the vote.

We plunged straight into the life of the station. In February Susan was taken on by the DC as a temporary secretary and typed judgements for the magistrate. Her first case concerned embezzlement by the Ankole Native Government's Assistant Treasurer and was a sharp introduction to Runyankore names. She enjoyed her jobs not just for the money but for the picture she received of what was happening in the district.

From 7 to 15 March I went on my first safari to saza (county) Bunyaraguru, some of which included the Ankole part of the Queen Elizabeth National Park. Towards the end of the safari I returned to Mbarara and took the whole family back to Bunyaraguru. Susan was allowed off work on the Saturday morning, and we joined John Savage, the game warden, in the park. I had work to do on Saturday so we toured the park, visiting fishing villages. We were late going to the

Christmas 1960

camping site and in the dusk I assumed that I would see any animals in good time to stop. It was nearly not true. The dark grey of elephants is difficult to spot, and I slid to a stop just behind an elephant crossing the road. His backside filled our windscreen. Luckily, he did not turn on us but trotted off. We also met a hippo, but saw him in good time. The boys loved sleeping in a tent, and rather to our surprise, the only animals we heard during the night were monkeys. We rose at 5.30 for a search for game. There were masses of kob, topi and elephants. At 9.00, when we were about to go back to the camp and had given up hope of seeing lions, we came across two up a tree. When we got close

Mbarara club, 1996

in the Land-Rover, one left, but the other, a lioness, was sleepy and indifferent to our presence. John took some fine photos. When the Land Rover was taken close to the tree she came down and lay in the grass near us, gazing at us with her beautiful golden eyes. After breakfast we broke camp and went looking for more game for John to photograph. We returned home tired, dirty but pleased.

I applied in March for a licence for a Mannlicher 8mm rifle which I had bought from the estate of someone who had died. Seventy cartridges came with the gun. The firearm licence was granted on 4 April, together with a game licence. The reason for buying the rifle was that I would be touring in areas with plenty of game, and game meat would make an agreeable variation for meals. I did not bother 'sighting' the rifle before taking it out for the first time, on safari in saza Nyabushozi, a sparsely populated area in the east of Ankole. At the end of the day's work I went out with Susan, my interpreter and two local guides. We soon found a small group of impala at a shootable distance. I stood up in the Land-Rover. The others watched in pleasurable anticipation of meat for their next meal. My first shot missed. My second missed. The impala leapt away, and the watchers gestured in irritation. How could I have missed such an easy target? I suspect that I did not have a real desire to kill them. The problem did not arise again, as my rifle was stolen shortly afterwards and I did not buy another. My only consolation was a pro-rata refund of my game licence fee over a year later, in July 1961.

Each year a regatta was held near the fishing village of Katunguru on the Kazinga Channel, dividing Ankole and Toro. This area lay in the Queen Elizabeth National Park. The regatta was organised by the local chiefs, and an ADC was sent to make sure the arrangements were in order. A team of European officials was entered for the canoe race. In 1960 it took place in early May and I was given responsibility for overseeing it. We went as a family and stayed in Mweya, the game park lodge. It was an enjoyable occasion, and overseeing involved getting the teams to the starting point more or less on time.

We had left our house under the care of our servants. As we were returning to Mbarara we were met by a police officer, who told us that our house had been burgled. The thieves had forced apart the bars on

Katunguru Regatta (photo: Peter Herbert)

the sitting room windows and gone straight to the bedroom, as nothing in the other rooms was touched. They stole Susan's jewellery, including a lovely Victorian pendant inherited from her grandmother; the loss still upsets her. They also stole my gold Hunter given to me by a relative for my twenty-first birthday, the Mannlicher rifle, sheets, the jackets of two suits and my Authentics blazer, as well as some good shirts bought on leave. It looked as if they had lain on our bed. The servants had not raised the alarm. The police said the thieves came from a Muslim village on the outskirts of Mbarara and, as Miriam came from the same village, they thought there might have been collusion between the thieves and our servants. The European officer in charge of the investigation did not inspire confidence. He said that the police knew where the jewellery was but they wanted to be sure they could seize it. They had watched the clothes being sold in a local market. As the days passed this continued to be the story. Then, suddenly, the thieves had taken it to Kampala, where it disappeared. Why did the police not carry out a thorough search of the place where they thought it was? We never got a proper answer; it was an incompetent investigation.

The next stage in this drama was the insurance claim. This involved two young assessors coming from Nairobi. They stayed in the Ankole Hotel, known as 'Melancholy Hotel', an adequate but depressing place. There was no argument over the amount to be paid for the jewellery, watch and gun. However, they claimed that the jackets would be assessed as half a suit. This would have left me less than the cost of new suits. Coming on top of the police dithering, this was too much. I was away so Susan went to the hotel and walked into the room occupied by the assessors. The senior one was lying on his bed in his underpants. His suit, of an electric blue, was on a chair. Undeterred, Susan went for him about the suits, pointing out that his suit trousers on their own would not be much use. She picked up his trousers and threatened to remove them. At a disadvantage, he gave way. The cheque from the insurance company arrived shortly afterwards. I greatly admired Susan's courage, or, perhaps, fury.

1961: WORK PATTERN

My work developed a pattern. 1961 gives an idea of the range of duties. Most months there was a formal safari. Every month I spent two days visiting the resettlement area. These trips were in addition to my responsibilities in the district headquarters.

The saza toured up to August, when refugees and elections took much of my time, were Bunyaruguru, Shema, Kashari and Nyabushozi. The miscellaneous tasks included marking the National Park boundary in Bunyaruguru (February), five days in June and two in July running law courses and, in June, paying compensation connected with a road programme and conducting a preliminary murder enquiry.

Month	On tour	Elections	Refugees	Resettlement	Misc.	Total
January	14	–	–	2	–	16
February	4	2	–	2	2	10
March	3	9	–	2	–	14
April	Local leave 1 to 23 April			2		2
May	8	–	–	2	–	10
June	–	1	–	2	7	10
July	3	–	–	7	2	12
August	4	–	–	2	–	6
September	–	–	0	2	–	0
October	–	–	14	2	–	16
November	–	3	2	2	3	10
December	–	9	–	2	–	11

RESETTLEMENT

The resettlement schemes were designed to populate the open places in the north-east of Ankole. The theory was that human habitation helped to prevent the spread of tsetse fly, which caused trypanosomiasis in cattle. Tsetse fly were spreading northwards, a serious problem in an area where cattle were an important element in the agricultural economy. Ankole cattle, with their enormous horns, were attractive but formidable, at least in appearance. The presence of game encouraged the spread of the fly so the tsetse control teams shot game and sprayed the trees and bushes. In 1960, for instance, they shot in Ankole, Bunyoro and Lango 3,750 bushbucks, 2,737 duiker and 1,222 reedbuck, as well as seven lions and six leopards.

The resettlement scheme was a success. I inherited the arrangements operated by Peter Herbert, who went on home leave in April 1960. One area, Nyansimbo, was almost filled so my time was spent opening up the Bygera valley (and later the Kakinga valley). The settlers, known as Banyaruanda, came from the overcrowded parts of Kigezi district in the south-west of Western province. There was no compulsion; they had to be persuaded. The attractions of moving were considerable. We provided a lorry to carry them and their possessions to the resettlement area, which was divided into plots. Some plots were set aside for schools and churches; another as a village headquarters, to which a muruka (parish) chief would be appointed when there were a significant number of settlers. Roads were made. Incomers were also given rations for several months, implements and seed to work the land. A few settlers left; most stayed.

In 1960 Hugh Fraser, who had been DC Kigezi, and I went to Kisoro, on the Congo border, to hold a meeting to recruit settlers. Susan's sister, Barbara Hastings, who was staying with us, came as well. After a night in the Kisoro Hotel we climbed Mfumbiro, the extinct volcano straddling the border. We hoped to see gorillas. In the event, we found their 'camps' but nothing of them. We did get to the top, though, climbing through giant heathers and lobelias.

I enjoyed visiting the resettlement area. There was a special pleasure in seeing a piece of not particularly attractive land providing homes and support for people who had earlier been suffering the effects of land starvation. Visits to the resettlement areas also gave me the opportunity to get out into the district. Susan and the boys came on some of my

Ankole cattle (photo: Peter Herbert)

visits. We would send the Land-Rover ahead so that the tents would be ready for us and Salatieri preparing our first meal. He was as good a cook on safari as at home. At first his 'stove' was three or four large stones round a fire. Later we bought a two-ring paraffin stove. Over the stove his 'oven' would be placed. This was a large paraffin can with one end cut to form a door. In this container he roasted anything, from chickens to pieces of beef and pork. On one occasion, when camping in the resettlement area, we sat outside our tent in the evening watching elephants moving slowly across the low valley in front of us. We also saw varieties of buck grazing. The elephants were a problem, as they enjoyed eating the settlers' crops and had to be moved on by the game rangers. On one visit we all stayed in the house of the officer in charge of a prison on the Toro border. It was a strange place, out in the country, and we did not take to the European officer. His daughter lived with him in her holidays from school and had an ayah/companion. At the end of our brief stay, Salatieri told Susan firmly that it would not be proper for her to go there again. So we did not stay there again, and in any case preferred camping.

Kisoro resettlement meeting (with Hugh Fraser)

When I left, responsibility for resettlement was handed to Jonathan Byamugisha, another ADC. My handover notes give a flavour of what was involved.

1. Policy

Basically the policy is to settle the Kakinga valley and then move to the east. There is doubt whether it will be possible to settle the Olyubu valley because of the elephant concentrations but it will be possible to start on what the Director of Tsetse Control calls the eastern arm of the Kakinga and is locally called the Kakere valley.

2. Finance

There will be sufficient funds this year from unused funds from other schemes. Following the recent rise in porters' pay an application for an extra £1412 was made. I have as yet no information about funds for 1962/63 and have written asking about this. Assuming the same rate of settlement I estimate the same amount as last year plus an extra £3000 to cover the increase in porters' wages ie £9000.

3. Law

You should read the Resettlement Bye-Law. It will be necessary to get the Kakere valley put on the schedule of areas under the Resettlement Bye-Law and I will take preliminary action on this.

4. Rations

Rations are issued to settlers at the following rates:

	Adults	Children
Posho	30lbs per month	15lbs per month
Beans or Groundnuts	14lbs per month	8lbs per month
Salt	2lbs per month	nil

The porters are not permitted to receive rations following the recent increase in pay. They will ask about this. The Muruka [Parish] Chief, Mukungu [village] Chief and their families receive rations. So does the clerk and his family.

There are adequate rations for about a month at Nyansimbo. As the Kakinga area fills and settlement moves east, it would be worthwhile considering building another store at the Mukungu HQ at Kakinga.

5. Tools

These were checked on my last visit. There are some missing and the Gombolola [Sub-county] Chief is looking for them. The ledgers are also not satisfactory and I have given orders for others to be opened.

I have asked the Muruka Chief to send me a list of the tools to be written off and when this has been received you should get Bilali to bring the tools in and ask the DC to appoint a Board of Survey.

6. Transport

Each month the Muruka Chief sends in a list of settlers to be transported. The names should be entered in the Transport Programme book and a letter sent to the Gombolola Chiefs concerned. Whenever possible two settlers should share a lorry as it is too expensive to bring one settler on each safari and would take too long.

When the lorry is not being used to transport settlers it can be used for taking rations, building materials and culverts.

7. Present State of Affairs

a. The prizes need to be given for the Health competition at Bigyera. Perhaps the DC would like to do this. The Gombolola Chief wants to lay on a lavish feast but Resettlement funds may not be used for this. The prizes are a radio and battery which are in the store here (Mr de Souza knows about this) and prize winners are listed in the file.

b. All the plots in Nyansimbo have been taken and the area should be closed down as soon as all the settlers have received their rations. I have asked the Muruka Chief to submit a list of the settlers still to receive rations and for how long. When the area is closed the responsibility for the road and the compound porters will be transferred to the Ankole Native Government [ANG] and you should see the Omubiki [Treasurer] about providing funds.

c. The new area in the Kakere valley is just being opened up. A road is being built from the bottom of the valley upwards. I have shown on the map where I think the road should go and the area to be settled. It is important to remember the primary objective of settlement is to remove the bush in the valleys where the fly live. Settlement should not be allowed far out of the valley.

d. The roads in the Kakinga valley are complete except for culverting and I have ordered sufficient culverts from the ANG. The Gombolola Chief is supervising the marking out of plots (which measure 200yds by 200yds).

e. The coffee nursery is doing well and 50 trees have been distributed to each settler. The balance may be bought by people living in the resettlement area or nearby. It will be necessary soon to obtain more coffee seed from the Agricultural Dept.

f. There is a constant need to keep an eye on water supplies. As the bottom of the Kakinga valley is opened for settlement you should find water holes suitable for improvement. The same should happen in the Kakere valley.

8. Duties on Monthly Visits

a. Inspect the ration ledgers and check that the amount issued to settlers balances the amount in the store. Also see the record of stocks balances the amount in the store.

b. Check the nominal roll of settlers.

c. Check progress in the resettlement area – especially see that instructions are being obeyed and that the settlement rules are being followed.

d. Give instructions for the next month – these should be repeated in writing on return.

9. Monthly Reports

Monthly Reports have not been sent for some time now. They used to go to the Provincial Commissioner Western Province but perhaps the Director of Tsetse Control would still like them.

The Muruka Chief should send you a monthly statement of the number of new settlers and the number of plots occupied.

Chapter 10

Refugees

The Congo became independent on 30 June 1960, and the first Belgians to leave and come to Mbarara were the Provincial and District Commissioners from just across the border, on their way to Kampala. I spoke to the latter in the club. The admin officers were disgusted that these two officials should be the first to leave, and that the Belgians had made no effort to hand over properly to their Congolese successors. Law and order was left to the Congolese army. We heard that, at the administrative centres, all files and papers had been removed, and Congolese officials took over empty offices. He said the same chaos would happen in Uganda; I did not believe him. Uganda at that time was stable; there were contingency plans for any disorder; and we were working towards a smooth handover of power.

The effect of independence on the Belgian civilians was dramatic. As far as we could discover, no contingency plans for the Belgian population had been made for response to disorder. If they did exist, the Belgians did not know about them. Rumours and horror stories were believed; panic set in. A rush of refugees came through Mbarara on their way to Kampala and, ultimately, Belgium; official reports state that there were 3,280. The refugees had mostly abandoned their homes and possessions. In one case we heard of Arab ponies left in their field. One family arrived with a young child with only one shoe; they had left in such a panic that they did not look for the other. Many refugees were not well off. An exception were a couple whom Susan saw at the police station. They had arrived in the latest model of Land-Rover, she in beautifully cut slacks, he equally well dressed. The Land-Rover was full of expensive luggage, including a magnificent leopard-skin coat. She wore an array of fine jewellery. She told Susan, in perfect English: 'My dear, we have lost everything.'

Arrangements for the refugees' reception were quickly made in Mbarara. The refugees were required to hand in their guns at the police station. They were then given vouchers for petrol to take them to Kampala. As always in such situations, there were those who exploited it to make a profit. We identified a couple of men who took their vouchers but, instead of going to Kampala, returned to the Congo to collect anything moveable that they could carry, such as fridges. Their reasoning was that the situation in the Congo was not as bad as feared and that, as the goods had been abandoned, they could be taken. Some went round several times, collecting vouchers each time.

Some of the refugees stayed in Mbarara overnight. Their accommodation was two unoccupied government houses. The local branch of the Red Cross was responsible for the arrangements. Most wives agreed to help. The houses had to be cleaned every day and the beds made. They were often left in a disgusting state. Susan thought that the arrangements were wrong; it would be easier to house the refugees in peoples' houses. After cleaning up a particularly disgusting mess, she went to Beaden Dening, the acting DC, because she thought he would listen to her. He did not accept her point, but word of what she had done reached the three Red Cross ladies who had been organising the accommodation. By chance one was the wife of the police officer who had investigated our burglary. They took umbrage. It so happened that they were all strong members of the local CMS/Native Anglican Church, and Susan was convinced that this influenced their attitude to her. We went ahead with having people to stay in our house.

The only couple to come out in good order were the American representative of Goodyear Export and his wife, Bonnie and Bill Jung, from Bukavu. We put them up. He said that his company had laid down a number of trigger events to which responses had been agreed. He had prepared for departure and they had their luggage ready. When the moment came they paid their servants six months' wages to look after the house (with their belongings upstairs). They recounted awful stories of how the Belgians talked about their servants to their face, referring to them as 'singes' (monkeys). They were so disgusted by this conduct that they were not prepared to entertain Belgians in their house.

Their stories echoed one told to Susan in the early 1950s by Mary Tew (later, she married Jimmy Douglas and, among other appointments, was Professor of Social Anthropology at University College London) who had been carrying out anthropological research in the Congo. She was appalled by the way priests and nuns treated the Congolese and was so concerned that she told Archbishop David Mathew, the Apostolic Delegate to West and East Africa. He heard her in silence and, after a long pause, said: 'They will be killed and cooked and eaten, and it will serve them right.'

The next refugees came from Rwanda, which was due to become independent on 1 July 1962. There had long been hostility between the Tutsi, the cattle aristocracy, and the Hutu, the agricultural peasantry. The Belgian administration had favoured the dominant though numerically smaller Tutsi. The approach of independence encouraged the Hutu to try to reverse this situation, and attacks began to be made on Tutsi. The result was that, by August 1961, Tutsi refugees started to cross the border into Ankole in considerable numbers. At first they kept close to the border but we set up a camp at Oruchinga in saza Rwampara. This consisted of an administrative centre surrounded by their traditional temporary grass huts, which the Tutsi erected as they moved about with their herds of cattle. A number moved to the camp but many stayed near the border. Later, in 1962, the policy was adopted of moving them from the border to the camp at Oruchinga and another at Nakavali. The grass huts greatly shocked an American lady journalist who visited the camp. Without understanding the problem or the Tutsi way of life, she was highly critical of the arrangements for the refugees.

Arrangements for coping with the refugees took a considerable amount of effort. These were assigned to me in addition to my other duties. In September I spent six days at the camp and in October fourteen days, including showing the chief minister, Benedict Kiwanuka, round it. Towards the end of October Ian Sanderson was sent to Ankole to work on the refugee problem, so, in November, I spent only two days at the camp.

There were reports of cross-border incidents involving both Tutsi and Hutu. In April 1962 the US State Department claimed that the Tutsi were receiving help from Ankole. The Colonial Office response was that there was no evidence of this but the governor's comments (in fact written by Christopher Powell-Cotton, a former Provincial Commissioner of Northern Province then working in Entebbe) were: a company of King's African Rifles was on the border; one raid had

Oruchinga refugee camp: administration centre

174

involved Tutsi from Ankole; the refugees would be moved to the camps; and half the refugees probably came just for the food, which had so far cost £100,000. A rumour circulated in the administration that Frank Kalimuzo was involved in some undisclosed way with the Tutsi as he had Tutsi connections. In April a raid was made into Uganda by a European and three Africans, in which two men thought to be helping the Tutsi were killed. By the end of June 1962 there were 49,316 registered refugees with 19,976 head of cattle.

The contracts for feeding the refugees were let locally and were much sought after by the Asian traders. I sat on the Ankole District Tender Board awarding the contracts, which came up regularly as the scale of the problem increased. One result was an attempt to bribe me. The family had gone into Mbarara for shopping. I was approached by one of the traders carrying a roll of fine tweed suiting. He thrust it into my arms. I handed it back. He made another attempt. I again refused to accept it. So he put it in the arms of Adrian, who was standing nearby. I removed it from a bewildered Adrian. In the end the trader accepted defeat.

Oruchinga camp: a new section

On one occasion we visited the camp with the Community Development Officer's wife, who was the head of the local Red Cross. She wanted to give the refugees clothes and food. She handed one of the mothers a nappy. Looking back, she saw that the mother had put it on her head as a scarf. The wife returned, took it off the mother's head and put it round the baby's bottom. She then moved on and, looking back, we saw that the mother had again put it round her head. The small cans of Heinz baby food received the same lack of respect. The contents were thrown on the ground so that the tins could be converted into cups. A simple lesson! Find out first what people really need.

Chapter 11

Politics and Religion

Ankole had a history of religious friction. There was an uneasy neutrality between the White Fathers (in historical terms the 'French') and the Church Mission Society/Native Anglican Church (the 'English'). This division appeared in many aspects of life in Ankole and was a central element in the political scene. For many years the balance of power in the District had lain with the Protestants. During my time there were some significant changes.

The first was the success of the Democratic Party (DP), the party supported by Catholics, in the Eishengyero (District Council) elections held on 9 November 1960. The sixty-five members of the Eishengyero were for the first time to be directly elected, with a chairman elected from the members instead of being ex officio the chief minister, the Enganzi. At the same time the Enganzi was to be appointed by the Omugabe (The King of Ankole) on the recommendation of an appointments board and with the consent of the Governor. The DP won thirty-six seats to the Uganda People's Congress's (UPC's) twenty-eight with one independent, who later joined the DP. There were allegations in gombolola Musale in saza Kajara about unqualified voters. The losers, the UPC, complained, and there were enough irregularities for the majority of forty-two to be put in doubt. So the election was rerun from the point of the nomination of candidates. There were similar complaints about the election in a gombolola in saza Nyabushozi. Voting took place on 22 February 1961. The count was still close in gombolola Musale and there were again irregularities. So a third election took place there on 4 July 1961. I had proposed that, to ensure that no fraud took place, the chiefs should identify all the electors as they collected their ballot paper. I then went ill, and heard later that voting went long into the night as the procedure was slow to operate. It was hard on the ADC, Robin Tamplin, I think, who had to supervise my arrangements.

After the election Basil Bataringaya, later a minister who was murdered, was elected chairman. The UPC members were virtually excluded from the Eishengyero committees. The DP majority then decided, without giving notice, that the regulations for the choice of Enganzi should be changed, so that he was elected, not appointed. The UPC walked out. In December a meeting was held to consider the government's response to the request to amend the regulations. Again the UPC walked out. The DP passed a vote of no confidence in the Enganzi. Although the term of office of the current Enganzi, N. K. Nganwa, expired a month after the convening of the new Eishengyero, he was reappointed by the Omugabe for a further four years on the advice of the appointments board. The DP then boycotted the traditional installation ceremony of the Enganzi. The matter did not rest there. The DP continued to press for change. Eventually Nganwa retired and John Kabaireho, a Catholic, was appointed.

Being a Catholic only impinged occasionally on my work as an ADC. In January 1961 I toured saza Shema. Before the tour I had been visited at home by Basil Bateringaya and a DP member of the Eishengyero full of complaints about how the elections were being run there. In the event I spent a great deal of time hearing complaints from all directions. As Susan wrote in a letter at the time, 'Shema was full of complaints.' One day I held a meeting from early in the morning until the evening.

At one gombolola headquarters when checking the court records I noticed that a group had been remanded for a trivial offence. I asked about it. It so happened that some of the group were at the headquarters and complained about their treatment. It became apparent to me that they were being remanded for political rather than criminal reasons so that they could not take part in the election process. They were members of the DP in a mainly UPC gombolola. I said they should be released on bail. The result was a letter of complaint to the DC about my actions. I still have the letter. In my address to the meeting I had explained the problems over the appointment of the Enganzi. This, combined with the release of those on remand, produced the letter. One paragraph gives a flavour of it:

> He enquired very much about the DP people and he is very much interested in their party. Without a doubt he is a DC of the DP in the whole of Ankole.

The only other attempt to involve my Catholicism was by a young White Father who had shot more than his quota of animals under his game licence. He tried, though not very hard, to persuade me to intervene with the Game Warden, John Mills. I refused, and he left with a shrug of his French-Canadian shoulders.

The White Fathers' bishop was Jean-Marie Ogez, an intelligent and liberal-minded Frenchman. We liked him a lot. He had been appointed to Mbarara in 1959, as his obituary put it, 'because of a particular difficulty which had arisen there. Fresh blood was needed, it was felt, to put an end to a certain amount of friction which had grown up between different groups of missionaries.' The obituary referred to a failure to agree on the spelling of Runyankore. In fact the trouble lay in the large number of unimpressive and conservative priests. The result was few African priests. Ogez's task was to bring forward African priests who could later be considered for appointment to bishop. When we complained to him about the attitude of some of the priests, he said that one of his first actions had been to retire or move the most reactionary priests. We attended his impressive silver jubilee celebrations in July 1960 in the presence of other bishops.

Bishop Ogez

The narrow-minded attitude of the White Fathers in the Mbarara parish affected us as a family. Before we arrived a fundraising event was held to raise money for the repair of the roof of the Catholic church, and it was supported by all the station. When the Native Anglican Church wanted to raise money for their church, a whisky-drinking Catholic priest from Edinburgh attached to the White

Fathers, said it was not acceptable for Catholics to raise funds for a Protestant church. We agreed with reluctance, but provided a crèche in our house so that mothers could work at the fete.

The same approach was applied to our children. Adrian was given the part of a shepherd in the club's nativity play. He was thrilled as he was to have a real sheep. It was performed one night in the club without any problem and he led his sheep. The next performance was in the Native Anglican church. When the White Fathers' parish priest heard about this, he came to see us. He said that if Adrian took part it would cause scandal to his African parishioners who would not understand how we could allow our son to enter a Protestant church and say the 'Our Father'. Foolishly, we agreed, to Adrian's disappointment. We should have ignored the priest completely, but times then were different and we felt we had to support him.

Another example involved a marriage at the CMS mission. We went to the church and found a Catholic couple, Maurice Phelan, the magistrate, and his wife, Joyce, standing at the entrance to the church. When we suggested that we should sit together, they said that they had consulted the parish priest and been told not to attend. They felt that they should put in an appearance but would not go into the church for the service. We went in, to their surprise. Our behaviour was reported to the White Fathers!

We made up for our earlier disobedience by Susan agreeing to play the part of Mary Magdalen in the Easter play in 1962. She dyed her hair auburn. The dye was obviously strong, as her hair became redder as time passed. It was still deep red when we returned to the UK in July.

ELECTIONS

The political atmosphere had changed during our UK leave in 1959. Rapid moves towards independence continued and, for me, dominated the rest of my time in Uganda. The constitutional committee under

John Wild reported in December 1959 and submitted a supplementary report in March 1960, setting out the recommended constituencies. There were six in Ankole.

The next general election took place on 24 March 1961. In Ankole the detailed arrangements were the responsibility of Robin Tamplin, a senior ADC. The process began in July 1960, with pre-registration (of voters) tours to explain the preparations for the election. Registration took place between 8 August and 3 September. The application forms, which had to be checked by ADCs, were taken to a large hall near the DC's office for typing in preliminary registers. Susan was one of the typists. When the preliminary registers had been issued, there was a period for claims (that a name had been omitted from the register, or objections to a name included in the register). There were few claims; I dealt with only five in saza Buweju.

The next stage was the selection and training of some 1,500 polling staff, and the choice of polling stations, often in schools. There were 465. Each polling station had to be visited. In August I spent three days visiting polling stations and six checking registration; in September nine days on both. Inspecting potential polling stations involved walking into some of the more remote parts of the district. Saza Buweju was a hilly area, very much on its own. The saza chief, a delightful and intelligent man, was in fact the hereditary ruler of the saza. One day a party of local chiefs and I had just finished climbing a steep hill, heading towards a distant polling station, when we met two young boys. They fell to their knees in front of me. I was both amazed and amused. What was the reason? The gombolola chief told me that the boys thought I was a White Father. Presumably they were the only white people who normally visited the area, which was predominantly Catholic. Given the length of our walk and climb, I was not surprised, but it said something about the White Fathers.

At the beginning of March 1961 I gave two courses to staff who would be working in saza Igara and Buweju. For the elections I was made returning officer for North West Ankole, which comprised saza Bunyaruguru and Buweju, and three gombolola each from saza Igara and Mitoma. The candidates were Abbas Balinda, UPC, whose symbol was a hand, and Basil Bataringaya, DP, whose symbol was a hoe. I was concerned about the election and wrote on 5 March to Susan's mother:

> I have at last finished a terrible run of safari but of course the elections are now onto us. I am most alarmed at the election staff (about 1500) as they look as if they are likely to make a hash through either inefficiency or bigotry. I only hope that no one presents an election petition. On the surface it looks as if the DP will win: Nabeta, the Minister of Works, leaving the UPC for the DP is one sign. The gains in the District Council elections (for the DP) is another.

I must have been feeling jaded. The election passed off well and there was no petition. In North West Ankole Bataringaya won comfortably. The enthusiasm for elections may be gauged by comparing the number of registered voters (211,847) with the number who cast their votes (197,796). Only 14,951 did not vote. The DP won four seats and the UPC two.

One manifestation of the move towards independence was the need to introduce the wives of prominent Ugandans to some of the responsibilities they would have to take on. One was giving parties. So Susan was asked to tell a group about how to give a sundowner. They were also anxious to learn about the arrangements for eating in public. So Susan went home, collected cutlery and showed them how to lay a table.

In June 1961 the Uganda Relationships Commission under Lord Munster reported. It had been tasked to examine the relationship between the central government and the other authorities in Uganda. The problem of the position of Buganda within Uganda dominated the report. The report stated (para. 125):

> Buganda has always been treated as a native state with its own system of government. The three other kingdoms have been governed more directly as districts within the same framework as the Protectorate has devised for all the other parts of the country, whether Kingdoms or not. Toro, Ankole and Bunyoro are native

Typing the election registers

states in the sense that they have hereditary rulers with their own councils; but their councils count as ordinary district councils for Protectorate purposes. They therefore occupy an ambiguous position, being neither full native states nor ordinary local authorities.

The report described them as having a semi-federal position: they were administered as districts but had separate agreements with the British government. The negotiations between the Governor and the Ankole delegation on Ankole's constitutional position continued into May 1962 – that is after self-government on 1 March 1962. The final agreement, forty one pages long, was signed in August.

The Munster report (para. 472) set out clearly the problems involved in agreeing the new constitutional arrangements.

Uganda has arrived at a turning-point in her history: a colonial regime accustomed to leisurely development is having to compress a decade of constitutional progress into a few months. It is, we believe, commonly accepted that this pace is dictated by events both in Africa and in the rest of the world, rather than by what is administratively best for Uganda. Our task is to endeavour to help both politician and administrator to do the best possible job in the time allowed. In many matters we have had to compromise between the ideal and the practical.

As the overall aim of the government was a unitary state, the position of Ankole was fudged. The position of the Omugabe was recognised, and within defined areas the Eishengyro could pass laws, but in general Ankole was firmly within a unitary state.

The report also dealt with the position of the Provincial and District administration. It recommended that most of the DC's responsibilities should be removed so that districts worked directly with the ministries. DCs had residual duties relating to law and order and a vague responsibility for 'attending to complaints and giving general assistance'. Hugh Fraser sent a note of guidance to ADCs (annex 1).

During this time the four rulers held periodic meetings. In 1962 it took place in Mbarara. I think it coincided with the Omugabe's party on 1 January. I was interested to see the rulers and was particularly struck by the way the Kabaka, the ruler of Buganda, was treated by his staff, who in his presence moved about on their knees with fixed smiles on their faces. Perhaps such an approach was well known to officials who worked in Buganda, but it was strange in Ankole.

In September 1961 the constitutional conference was held in London. It provided for another general election, which took place on 25 April 1962. This time as ADCI I was responsible for the arrangements in Ankole. The number of registered voters increased to 242,307 and on the day 208,720 voted, an 86.1% turnout.

In my report to the elections supervisor in Entebbe I commented on the activities of the political parties:

It is extremely hard to assess the extent and effectiveness of party organisation unless one has made a point of investigating it, so I can only make general comments based on my own limited knowledge and the reports of Assistant Returning Officers who were in charge of constituencies.

In both parties political organisation at a low level appeared to be well developed, even if some of the local agents were of low calibre. A measure of the success of party organisation at village level was the paucity of political activity immediately before the election, which indicated that voters had made up their minds for whom they were going to vote and saw no reason for attending political meetings, and the high percentage of voters who turned up on polling day.

On election day I received the impression that the UPC had put more of their resources into Ankole than the DP. They had more cars available for visiting villages to root out supporters, for carrying the aged to polling stations and for watching assistant returning officers at work, especially during the collection of boxes after voting. In the borderline constituencies, such as West Ankole and South East Ankole, reports suggest that the UPC had more agents at work in the villages. I do not consider that this kind of activity had any marked effect on results.

Both political parties had the liveliest suspicions concerning the honesty of Assistant Returning Officers and, as you know, were most alarmed about the collection of ballot boxes after voting, especially as agents were not allowed to accompany Assistant Returning Officers. In many areas the UPC had provided cars to follow Assistant Returning Officers. This was true even in the wilds of Nyabushozi! While sympathising with their concern, I think that it would have had to be a very determined Assistant Returning Officer to tamper with the boxes after a long day's work and with the prospect of eventually delivering the boxes to the constituency headquarters any time up to 5.00 a.m.

One reason for the lack of party activity before the election was, I am sure, the religious loyalties: in general Catholics voted DP, Protestants UPC. However, the results showed a swing to the UPC, in line with the swing throughout Uganda. One local influence which resulted in the DP losing the seat in South East Ankole was the UPC candidate, a Muslim who was able to attract the considerable

Muslim and Baganda vote. He won by 161 votes. This meant that the UPC and DP each won three seats.

Shortly after the results were announced one of the candidates, an unsuccessful one, visited me at home. As we sat talking over a beer, he said that he thought the elections had been fair. This was my view, but it was good to have it supported.

All elections have their comic episodes. The staff effort in running them was immense. All government officials were involved in some way. The only one to refuse to help personally was Douglas Jones, the Tsetse Control Officer working in saza Nyabushozi. He pleaded a tour of South West Masaka. He went on to say that his experience of the rural population in Nyabushozi, and their response to his enquiries about their knowledge of the political parties, made him question the desirability of the elections. He asked to be excused from being an Assistant Returning Officer. I took the strict line, saying that I needed fifty-nine Assistant Returning Officers and needed him. Douglas appealed to Hugh Fraser, who accorded him conscientious objector status! Douglas put his Land-Rover and driver at my disposal.

The other incident which could have been tragic concerned an Assistant Returning Officer travelling in saza Buweju, a mountainous area. His Land-Rover overturned down the slope below a bulungi bwansi road (a road built by local people's voluntary labour for the good of the local area). Trees stopped the fall and no one was hurt, and local people quickly lifted the Land-Rover onto the road. The officer was the same one who had been involved with a drunken presiding officer and an enraged hippo in the Queen Elizabeth National park during the 1961 election. He asked for a stationary job for the next election.

In mid-May I handed over responsibility for residual work on the election to Jonathan Byamugisha. Emmanuel Wakhweya was passed responsibility for applications for firearms certificates (my handover note is at annex 2).

Chapter 12

Social Life and End of Tour

I mentioned earlier the club and the sports that took place around it. By 1961 I was the tennis member responsible for matches and tournaments. There was also a play reading group, which was well supported. In early 1962 a full production of *Blithe Spirit* was put on. Susan was Madame Acarti, a part she enjoyed enormously. They took the play to the mining town of Kilembe. By another of life's curious links, the producer, Tony Wilson, turned up in the Helen's Bay Players when we were in Northern Ireland in the late 1970s.

Social engagements were for the most part either a Sunday curry lunch or dinner. The curry lunches began with a great many gins and were accompanied by beer. Susan found them a trial. The dinners were more varied than in Soroti because the stock farm just outside Mbarara slaughtered and sold its stock. Good-quality meat was therefore available. The usual cut given at dinners was pork fillet but, thanks to Salatieri's skill, people coming to dinner with us did not know what they would be given. The ritual of dinners in Uganda was well established, and after the men had risen from the table they 'saw Africa', the pleasurable custom of peeing in a line into your host's flower beds. The women retired to their hostess's bedroom, where the usual topic of conversation was the problems with their servants, in particular the iniquities of ayahs.

We were spared an ayah in Mbarara, as the boys went to school. Adrian attended the European Primary School, run by any wife qualified to teach who happened to be posted to Mbarara. The result was that he was way behind when we returned to the UK. Susan was secretary of the school and was accused, unjustly, by the chairman of not putting enough effort into her post. A row followed. That night we met him and his wife at dinner at the Sandersons. There was no mention of the row and we managed to get through the whole dinner without speaking to them directly, but it was the end of our friendship.

Nick went to a nursery school in the town run by a European for the children of the shopkeepers. He was one of only two European children there, but he enjoyed it. When we went shopping in the evening he would disappear behind the counter of whichever shop we were in, to the sound of much giggling. The boys' better health was a great relief. Nicholas had one scare: nephritis in 1961, which required a trip to Nakasero Hospital in Kampala. Luckily, there was no lasting damage to his kidneys. Susan also had to go to Kampala for medical appointments. On one occasion in November 1961 she took three women on a day trip. They left in the early morning and in Nyabushozi saw a pair of lions lying on the edge of the road. The passengers shopped while Susan was at the hospital having a minor operation. She then drove them back to Mbarara, altogether a journey of over 300 miles. The newly constructed road between Mbarara and Masaka made it possible.

The shops had a reasonable range of goods, certainly all the basics. The most attractive was run by Aziz Virani, with its stock of attractive gifts and useful equipment. One great bonus was the ability of all the various workshops to improvise. The Citroën ID19 was a complicated piece of machinery and we had on a number of occasions to summon a mechanic from Kampala to correct some fault. After a trip on rough roads and some bush driving, the mechanism which varied the clearance broke. The car just collapsed. Rather than have the car removed to Kampala we had it taken to an Asian workshop in Mbarara. With great skill the owner welded back into place the broken piece of the ball socket. It survived until we sold the car in London.

There continued to be a constant flow of visitors to stay: people going on leave or on transfer whose possessions had left and who wished to avoid the hotel or government rest house; or official visitors, such as the bandmaster, Mr Tonks, of the King's African Rifles band in July 1961. A frequent visitor, sometimes for as long as a week, was Dick LeFanu, the British Council representative from Fort Portal. He seemed to spend his time giving talks to schools and colleges on the British constitution or showing films, frequently *Henry V*. His was a fairly relaxed routine and he could not understand why I could not play tennis with him in the afternoon during working hours. When his wife Anne was away he would bring their West Highland bitch, once when she was about to pup. She did so, on a bed in our spare room. Sometimes he would escort a British Council group. In July 1961 he came with Rosalind Fuller, who mimed with great skill, in the manner of Ruth Draper, Shakespeare plays and *The Young Visitors*. We gave a party in our house to mark her visit. As in Soroti we had an unexpected visitor, claiming, correctly, that he was a school friend from King's. He came to our door late in the evening after a long session at the club. When Susan went to the door and asked who it was, he replied: 'A white man!' When she opened the door he fell in. He said he would be off early next morning, which, seeing his condition, we doubted. However, he did leave before we were up.

A delightful place to visit in the district was Toni Nuti's Island. She had acquired an island in the middle of the river Kagara. On it she built a house and would put people up for the night. There was a footbridge to the island, though we heard later that it had been swept away and visitors were pulled over the water in a basket. We made a number of visits. The children loved it as Toni had a little civet kitten. We saw hippo browsing on the lawn at night, and the noise of the rushing water was magical. Susan's mother was a hit with Toni who asked, whenever we visited, when she would come again. Later, after we had left, she did go there on her own. On one occasion, with Hugh

Fraser, we used the island as the base for a search for rhino in Tanganyika. We had to wait until the grass had been burnt off. This involved crossing the Kagara at Kikagati, upstream, and driving about in the hope of finding them. We were lucky and saw them in a slightly alarming way. We had left the cars and walked towards the edge of a drop into a small bushy valley. Just below the edge were the rhino, two adults and a calf. As we looked down on them, they ambled off.

On one visit we met Toni Nuti's brother, who worked in Tanganyika. He was a hunter and died as a result of ignoring a basic rule when hunting buffalo. He thought he had killed one and approached it, leaving his rifle in his pick-up. The animal, which was only stunned, rose and gored him. He was taken to hospital in Kampala but died there.

In April 1961 we went on leave to the coast south of Mombasa staying at the Two Fishes, run by Mr and Mrs Fish (it used to be the Three Fishes when his mother was alive). The bedrooms were in separate thatched huts with a central bar and dining room. It was a few yards to the sea. The water was protected by the reef, and fishermen left their outriggers on the beach. I preferred sitting under the palm trees at the top of the beach but the children spent much of their time in the sea. Inland from the coast south of Mombasa was a game park. Its attraction for us were sable antelope. We went searching for them with friends. Following my instinct I went across country in our ID19 and found these beautiful animals. On the way back to Mbarara we bought a stock of basic food from Hassan Juma in Mombasa and two 'Bokhara' carpets in Nairobi (they were, of course, woven in Pakistan, but they have survived and are still decorative).

In June 1961 we sold our Chappell baby grand to Caroline Phillips in Fort Portal for £150. It was sad to see something go that had belonged to my mother in Malaya and Kenya, but it had suffered terribly on the journey from the UK and we reckoned that it would be easier to sell it in Uganda than in the UK.

On 17 October 1961 I wrote to Peter Allen, the Permanent Secretary in the Office of the Prime Minister, asking to remain in

Ankole until the end of my tour in June 1962 and telling him of my wish to retire with compensation at the end of leave in November 1962 (See annex 3). I think it reflected the views of Administrative Officers of my vintage. He replied accepting my requests. In November he sent a letter to Administrative Officers about the General Compensation Scheme. In it he put the arguments for us to remain in Uganda after independence. They were that a job in the UK would be less well paid (true, in my case, to begin with), be less interesting (not true, in my case) and that finding a satisfactory job up to the age of forty should not be difficult. Coming up to thirty, I was not persuaded. There seemed every reason to start looking for a new job as soon as possible. I was interested in a transfer to Hong Kong but it came to nothing, as did an application for an administrative post in Manchester University. I was also interested in the Foreign Office but the date for the exams coincided with our voyage to the UK; so that also foundered.

At the end of January 1962 I started to book a sea passage to the UK through Smith Mackenzie, the agents for Union Castle. We wanted to go via the Cape of Good Hope in June. The application for leave was submitted in early February. Then, on 9 February, my father died. My mother had sent a telegram saying he was seriously ill; another followed shortly after with news of his death and a request that I should go to Alderney to support her. He had been moving a delivery of coal to their coal bunker and suddenly been taken ill. He died, after three strokes, in the Mignot Memorial Hospital, which he had helped to set up. So I went to Alderney for two weeks at the end of February. My father had already been buried at sea off the little island of Burhou, which he loved and where he had helped to establish a small birdwatching centre (at that time the island was home to thousands of puffins). He was taken out in the Trinity House boat but my mother refused to accompany him. The weather was extremely cold but my mother had already given my father's clothes to charity. The only warm garment left was a duffel coat on the back of a door. Later, in the summer, we went to a little ceremony at which a memorial plaque to him was put up in St Anne's parish church. The wording was his and typical of him: 'A humble resident of this island for 13 years.'

Our last excursion as a family into the district was a couple of nights in the Kichwamba Hotel in saza Bunyaruguru. It was built in a dramatic position, on the edge of the cliff dropping hundreds of feet to the Queen Elizabeth National Park. It was a lovely place in which to say farewell to Ankole, but the visit had its downside as Adrian became ill and, when we took him to the excellent Seventh Day Adventist hospital not far away, he was diagnosed with jaundice.

Work continued as normal right up to our departure. The packing was a chore but past experience helped. There were farewell dinners, fourteen in a row, with pork fillet at every one. We decided to take the Citroën. So, after the main luggage had been collected for shipment to the UK through the government coast agent in Mombasa, we drove with Salatieri through Tororo, where we left him together with farewell presents, such as a coffee set. In Nairobi we stayed in the transit camp which government servants could use. Then on the direct road to Mombasa. It was not in marvellous condition and the dust was terrible. The Tudor House Hotel where we stayed was a welcome relief.

VOYAGE TO THE UK

The *Rhodesia Castle* was due to leave on 11 June but was a day late. The Citroën was not loaded until the last moment so we were able to use it in Mombasa. When it was loaded, by one of the great cranes lowering it into the hold, we watched with interest and apprehension. All was well, though it did receive a dent in Tilbury. The *Rhodesia Castle* was a single-class ship, and we had a large double cabin and the children a single on the other side of our bathroom. The air-conditioning was a great boon at night but it was so cold in the public rooms that we caught colds. Susan does not enjoy sea travel and was sick even before leaving Mombasa Harbour. The stop at Zanzibar enabled us to buy a small Zanzibar chest. We also found a taxi driver to take us round the island. He welcomed my upcountry Swahili – a contrast to American tour ship visitors?

The next stop was Biera. We had hoped for Lourenzo Marques. We then went down the South African coast to Durban, where we transferred to the *Athlone Castle*, an elderly two-class ship only three voyages from its retirement. We had expected to have less than a day in Durban but actually had a day and a half, so were able to go to the aquarium, where Adrian was terrified, to begin with, by the sharks swimming towards the underwater viewing window, and to the snake park.

The *Athlone Castle* was a shock. We were together in a cabin in tourist class. It was dirty and the steward surly. The ship was crowded with about 500 in tourist class, of whom 120 were children. There were only sixty-two in first class to Cape Town and thirty-seven afterwards, but they had most of the deck space. Walking around on deck was like walking down a crowded street. We tried to change to a better cabin but there were none. The only escape was to transfer to first, which one couple from Uganda did. Thinking of the future we refused to spend the extra fares. We and others complained to the Purser but the Captain made no effort to improve the situation.

After Durban we sailed overnight stopping at East London, Port Elizabeth, where we met Mike Searle, a fellow hockey Blue from Trinity, and Mossel Bay. For one of the overnight stages we saw a very pregnant woman come on board. Later we heard that, during the night, she had had the baby, who the Captain would baptise on the return voyage. It was the second time that she had deliberately had a baby on a British carrier – the previous time on a plane – in order to get British nationality for her children.

After we left Durban, Nicholas became ill. We thought it was another attack of nephritis but it turned out to be jaundice, caught from Adrian. By the time we reached Cape Town he was too unwell to leave our cabin and Susan had to spend most of the time with him. It was an uncomfortable experience, as there was nowhere to sit other than on the bunk beds. I got out one day for a long walk to Table

Mountain with Frank Holden, a Provincial Education Officer. The Holdens were congenial companions during the voyage.

Cape Town was chiefly memorable for the revolt of tourist-class passengers. A number, including ourselves, went to the Union Castle offices. A polite and sympathetic woman heard us out and promised to pass on all our complaints, which covered the filth, the wretched service from the stewards and the lack of space. We also tried to negotiate a change to a first-class cabin but to continue to eat in tourist class, but without success. There was a quick response to the complaints. The Captain had obviously been put on the mat. As Susan said in a letter: 'The Tourist Section is dripping with gold braid and soapy water.' We were also given more deck space. After we had left Cape Town the captain, in a speech at an evening event, spoke in a slightly grumpy way about people who had complained. For the rest of the voyage he made a point of attending tourist-class entertainments. After a stop in the Canary Islands, where we went on a tour of the volcanic mountains, we arrived in the UK and left almost immediately for Alderney to see my mother.

Crossing the line

After a period of relaxation I had to find a job. A house would have to wait until we knew where I was working. I went to the Colonial Office resettlement bureau. During my interview with its head, a retired Provincial Commissioner from Tanganyika, he explained in the gloomiest way that jobs were hard to get and I could well wait for months, but they would do their best. His assistant was a helpful lady, Miss Moore. A District Officer post was available in Swaziland and I could be recommended for it. Returning to Africa was attractive. The trouble was that it was a three-year contract and, although I negotiated for an extension to eleven years, the prospect of looking again for a job at forty-one was unappealing. Another voyage on a Union Castle ship so soon after the *Athlone Castle* was also a deterrent. So I turned it down. The post was taken by Hugh Fraser, my former DC. His description of what he actually did in Swaziland made me glad to have declined the post; but he was able to save a lot of money!

Interviews with Shell and the British Council were arranged. Shell turned me down because I was too old to fit into their career structure. The British Council also declined my services. They were

The Holdens and us with the captain

right; I was not their kind of person. I began the process of recruitment as a tax inspector and was asked if I would like my name put to MI5 and MI6. On 9 October Susan and I attended the Uganda Independence Day service in Westminster Abbey followed by the party in County Hall. The same month I was about to have an interview with GKN but decided to ask if MI5 and MI6 had turned me down. Miss Moore made enquiries and rang in some embarrassment to tell me that my file had been put away without action being taken. She promised to deal with it immediately. The resettlement bureau told me on 9 October that they had sent on my name. On 12 October I was invited to a preliminary interview with the Security Service (MI5). After a final board interview on 26 November I was accepted, and I joined on 31 December 1962.

Chapter 13

Conclusions

I look back on my time in Uganda as something special. It forced me to grow up quickly and taught me some hard lessons. One was to make me take care to understand regulations. I still remember with some embarrassment my failure to pass in time through the town council an increase in the rates for commercial properties. It required the intervention of the DC to persuade the non-official members to approve the increase retrospectively. We also made a number of very good long-term friends. I hope that, in return, I contributed a little to sound administration and the political development in Uganda.

Its subsequent history, until Yoweri Museveni took over as president, is sad and appalling. In 1962 John Champion and Mike Davies, both senior Administrative Officers, wrote a perceptive paper entitled 'Uganda – prospects following independence'. They saw the greatest threat coming from tribalism, mentioning in particular the differences between the Baganda and the northern tribes, from which a high proportion of the police and army came. They also feared that the attacks of the UPC on the DP might lead to the banning of the DP and the creation of a one-party state. In this connection Hugh Fraser, then working in the Ministry of Internal Affairs, wrote to me in September 1962:

Currently there is an assassination ploy being plugged by the wilder members of the UPC. I need hardly say it is the DP, plus those beastly catholic priests, particularly in Kigezi, who are responsible for this fiendish plot which involves smuggling of arms from Ruanda. Ben [Kiwanuka] has countered by asking the DPP to instigate a prosecution for criminal libel; one wonders what this presages after uhuru [freedom].

It is certainly true that the convenient and efficient division of the country into districts based on tribal divisions reinforced tribalism, but it is difficult to see how the country could have been administered in any other way given the size of the administration. I doubt if any British official foresaw just how quickly the government would become a brutal tyranny. Some of the public had imprecise fears. Not long before we left I was walking along a street in Mbarara when a man, whom I did not know, came up to me and asked: 'Who will look after us when you go?' To my later shame, I could only say that it was time for us to go and I was sure all would be well. What else could I say – that I had serious reservation about the survival of Westminster-style government? On safari people begged us not to go; one man was in tears.

Despite the horrors of Idi Amin and Milton Obote it was remarkable how Ugandans, a resilient and intelligent people, survived the bad times. Somehow many continued their education, and a great many managed to learn good English. During a visit in 1996 to the Roman Catholic centre in Madera, outside Soroti, I commented on the size of the girls' school. I was told that during the worst periods, when travelling around the country was dangerous, the nuns kept most of the girls in the school all the year and at the same time the school had continued to grow.

I have wondered if Uganda would have developed more peacefully without British rule. I have my doubts. Intertribal fighting would have continued. The 'lost counties' of Bunyoro, which the Banyoro considered to have been 'stolen' by the Baganda many years earlier, continued to be a running sore up to independence. In any case,

Uganda could not have remained a kind of human zoo isolated from the rest of Africa and the world. How, for example, would education and medical services have developed? So, what did British administration give to Uganda? First, a system of government which, at district level, still operates. During our 1996 visit to Mbarara I had hoped to be able to consult the district archives. As we stood outside the District Office, a young man came out and asked if he could help us. He said the records were in the Omugabe's former palace where the officer in charge of the Region (as the District is now called) worked. Time did not allow us to go there. The young man turned out to be an Assistant Regional Officer. In his approach and style he could have been an ADC of the past.

At a more basic level, the British provided stability. There were occasional disturbances but they had local causes and did not affect the country as a whole. Critics of colonial rule would do well to remember the far more serious disorders that occur in the UK. As a District Officer my impression was that people's basic needs are security, conditions that allow commerce to flourish and provide a reasonable standard of life, access to sources of water and electricity, and opportunities through education for people to better themselves. None of this is surprising, but a glance at the world shows that these conditions are not easy to achieve in many countries. My mother-in-law, Hazel Hastings, taught at Bwanda, a girls' school outside Masaka. She was a natural and imaginative, but unqualified, teacher. After a discussion with the girls in her class about the current state of Uganda, she asked them to write an essay on what the British had achieved. One girl wrote about the contrast between pre-British and British times. Hazel asked where she had obtained her information. It was from her grandmother. So Hazel asked the girl to question her grandmother about the main difference between the two periods. The girl reported that her grandmother had thought carefully and said 'the absence of fear' under the British. She went on to say that the chiefs had had power over life and death. Something as trivial as spilling a chief's beer could have resulted in losing one's hand.

Most Ugandans now have little if any knowledge of British rule. We were told during our visit in 1996 that 50% of the population was under twenty-one, and so much has happened in the country in recent years. This ignorance can be slightly comic. In Soroti Susan and I went to the former European Club, which was about to start as a nursery school. We looked at the swimming pool outside. The small amount of water in it was green. A boy who had been helping his mother to set up the school came up to us. We told him that we had helped to build the pool and it was sad to see it in such a state. His response was to demand why we had let it get into a mess. Susan then pointed to the house in which we had lived but he found it difficult to understand how we could have lived in Soroti. He had no idea of the age of the pool and, apparently, what had happened since it had been built.

By contrast, in Kampala we went with our hosts to have an evening drink at a hotel. We sat on the grass. I chatted to a man working at one of the universities in Kampala. He asked me about my interest in Uganda. I told him of my time as an ADC. He said that his father had been an Education Officer under the British and described it as 'our golden era'. On a visit to the Kabakas' tombs, something we had not done when working in Uganda, the man issuing tickets at the gate shut up shop and went with us to the tombs. I guess he was in his thirties. When talking about the tombs and the responsibilities of the women working there, he suddenly asked why the British had left so soon. I explained the international pressure and the wish of people to govern themselves, but he expressed regret at our departure. When I told Andrew Stuart about this encounter he dismissed it as just politeness. The Baganda are polite, but the question came out of the blue without preliminaries. So, presumably, it was something that concerned our guide. All I can deduce from these episodes is that, with some Ugandans, the British are remembered kindly. I was recently given an example of the welcome given to the British approach, this time to an army training team in Tororo in 1985 (annex 4).

One question often asked is whether we left too soon. I think the question should be: did we leave at the right moment for Uganda? It is not easy to judge the right moment but I think the answer has to be 'no'. The moment was not of our choosing. The increasingly educated and articulate middle class in the Empire demanded change. There was great international pressure, especially from the United States, one of whose long-term policies had been the dismemberment of the Empire. The UK was in dire financial straits and the government did not wish to cling to colonies just in order to prepare them better for independence.

So far as Uganda was concerned, independence should have come later. The rush through self-government to independence did not give enough time for politicians to become acquainted with the nature of government and administration, or the National Assembly to become used to a routine of business that allowed the new government to settle and the opposition to accept its role. It is hard to say whether a few more years would have made a difference but it might have prevented the excesses that followed Obote's first period of government.

The next question is whether more could have been done at an earlier stage to bring Ugandans into government service, particularly the provincial administration. John Kaboha and Frank Kalimuzo were in the first group of Ugandans to become full District Officers. There was a limit to the number of graduates, mainly from Makerere University but also from other universities, who could be recruited into the administration. There were significant demands from other departments of government. A number of Assistant Administrative Officers had been appointed but only a few were suitable for promotion. The problem had begun to be addressed in 1952, when a standing committee on the recruitment, training and promotion of Africans for higher posts was established under the chairmanship of John Wild. In 1954 the Ledbury Commission recommended a single unified civil service with common basic rates of pay but with inducement allowances for those recruited by the Colonial Office and the Crown Agents. In September 1955 the Public Service Commission was established administratively, and it was formally set up on 2 November 1957 by an Order in Council.

It was chaired initially by Sir Peter Gunning and, from early 1962, by Yusuf K. Lule.

The basic problem was that Uganda moved very quickly from an administered country to independence. Unlike India, where Indians had attended universities in Britain and had been in senior posts for many years, Uganda's education system was new. Although Makerere had its origins in 1922, it was only in 1949 that it became the University College of East Africa. It could not produce sufficient government officials for Uganda. Ugandans did go to other countries, especially the UK, for training but, again, there was insufficient time to train enough to take over the administration. It was not a question of abilities but of time. It would have required a very early and long-sighted programme of Africanisation, and until the 1950s the government of Uganda was not ready for such a programme.

With the approach of self-government and independence there was increasing pressure to recruit Ugandans. By the end of 1960 there were twenty-one Ugandan District Officers and cadets out of an establishment of ninety-five. There were also nineteen Ugandan Assistant Administrative Officers. A Public Service Commission recommendation not to recruit any expatriate district officers was implemented in 1960. In its report of 1961 the Commission stated that the records of all Assistant Administrative Officers had been reviewed and seven recommended for appointment as District Officers. At the same time, the governor had agreed special legislation to allow Ugandans to be promoted over better-qualified expats, who could then retire on compensation. In 1961 there were twenty-one such cases.

When we arrived in Mbarara, John Kaboha was one of the ADCs. After he left we were joined by Emmanuel Wakhweya and Jonathan Byamugisha. The former, who became finance minister under Amin, now lives in Bugisu, and, by one of life's chances, is connected to the Butiru Cheshire Home, which I visited several times up to 2000 as International Chairman of Leonard Cheshire. The last news I had of Jonathan was a posting in the Uganda mission to the United Nations shortly after independence. John Kaboha became a Permanent

Secretary but Obote refused to have him, probably as he was a Catholic, so he left to work first for UNICEF and then the Commonwealth Secretariat. So his abilities and experience were not used. As I wrote earlier, Frank Kalimuzo was murdered. A number of expat officers remained after independence but few for more than four or five years, and they could not make up for the shortage of sufficiently experienced Ugandan administrative officers. My generation of administrative officers left at or around independence.

In the period after independence was given to many countries in the empire, there was great hostility in the UK to our role as a colonial power. It was something to make apologies for. This was also the attitude of some senior British diplomats. As time passes, and under the influence of events around the world, particularly in Africa, this view is changing, and it is possible to make a cooler assessment of the empire, recognising its achievements as well as its failures. The lot of the ordinary person, whom District Officers tried to protect, has improved for some, but for many it has worsened. Perhaps academics and the public are coming to recognise that the stability of British colonial rule, and the gradual improvements achieved during it, did benefit the majority of people, and were in many ways something of value.

I am glad to have contributed, even to a limited extent, in preparing the way to independence for Uganda, a country for which Susan and I have great affection.

Annex 1: Guidance to ADCs on Changes to the Constitution

TO: All A.D.C.s   3rd April, 1962.

Notes for use in enkiko on recent changes
in the Constitution etc.

The following notes are provided for your speeches. If you think they are too complicated for a normal gombolola audience simplify as required. I shall use the same notes for my speeches to saza councils.

(a) Uganda having achieved self-government on the 1st March a new Constitution is now in force made by the Queen-in-Council. This Constitution is the one agreed on by all parties at the conference in London in October last.

(b) Self-government means that Uganda is now entirely responsible for its own affairs except for defence and relations with other countries, military affairs, internal security and control of the Police Force. These matters are still reserved for the Governor, although he has delegated his powers in respect of internal security and the Police Force to the Ministry of Home Affairs. He can take these powers back if necessary.

(c) Uganda is now ruled by a Cabinet presided over by the Prime Minister, and these Ministers make policy which all civil servants of whatever race carry out, including the D.C. and his officers.

(d) Apart from the duties mentioned above the Governor is now principally the Queen's representative in Uganda and has a very important task in helping to negotiate the final Constitution of Uganda before independence day on 9 October 1962. It does not necessarily mean that the final Constitution will greatly differ from the present one.

(e) One of the matters to be decided is the status of Ankole, including the demand of the Eishengyero and the Omugabe for federal status. It was agreed in London that the following matters should be guaranteed for Ankole both in the Constitution and in a new Ankole Agreement:

The position of the Omugabe;

Provision for Ministers;

The establishment of the Eishengyero;

The Omugabe's successors;

The boundaries of Ankole.

The new Agreement has not yet been signed until the question of federal status is decided. When it is made it can, however, last only until independence day and before then safeguards on these matters must be embodied in the Constitution of Uganda. The present intention is that it should be impossible to change any of these matters without a two-thirds majority of the Eishengyero confirmed by a two-thirds majority of the National Assembly. All these matters will have to be fully discussed and agreed. (N.B. Do not enter into any argument or discussions of the merit of the claim for federal status – simply say it is a matter for the Omugabe, the Eishengyero and the Secretary of State.)

(f) The changes immediately affecting people in Ankole are as follows:

(1) *Land*

The term 'Crown Land' is abolished and all land will be vested in an Ankole Land Board which will make policy for land in Ankole. It cannot, however, interfere with the rights of existing occupiers, nor can it interfere with mining. Furthermore the Minister of Lands will be able to give directions to the Board on matters of over-riding public interest. It is intended that the Board shall consist of not more than 8 members appointed by the Omugabe on the advice of the Eishengyero. It is possible that these matters may be somewhat varied by the Agreement.

This Land Board has not yet been set up. Meanwhile all land matters will be dealt with by the D.C.'s office as before, including T.O.L.s.

(2) *Police*

It is intended that Ankole shall have its own proper police force which will be trained and equipped properly and police the rural areas. This may take several years to accomplish because of expense and the time it takes to train. The Central Government police will continue to be responsible for towns and major crimes. Some of the existing A.N.G. police will be absorbed in the new Ankole police, others will be retained to help chiefs with minor duties.

(3) *Justice*

The courts will be reorganised either partly or altogether with effect from the 1st July, 1962. Instead of having a D.A.C., county courts and gombolola courts it is intended to remove chiefs from the courts and have professional judges instead. As these are recruited and trained they will take over the gombolola courts and one judge will probably do several gombololas. Appeals will be direct from these courts to the D.A.C. Court members will be abolished.

The D.C. has already ceased to have anything to do with native courts and a Native Courts Advisor, Western Region, has been appointed (P.O. Box 73,

Fort Portal). All appeals and petitions which formerly went to the D.C. must now be sent to him.

The D.C. and Saza Chiefs will no longer inspect court cases and books. This will be the duty of the Omuramuzi and his judges.

(4) *Administration*

There will be increased responsibility for the Ankole Native Government as follows:- (w.e.f. 1st July, 1962)

In addition to primary schools it will take over junior secondary schools, farm schools and rural trade schools.

It will take over increased medical responsibility including public health outside towns, dispensaries, health centres, aid posts and ambulances.

It will take over responsibility for all towns and trading centres except Mbarara.

The new Agreement might transfer more responsibilities but it does not seem likely as the Eishengyero has not asked for this.

These will certainly be an extra number of Ministers in the Native Government; this is still being negotiated in the new Agreement.

To run these extra services the Eishengyero will receive increased revenues by being allowed to impose graduated tax on non-Africans, by imposing rates on property in towns and trading centres except Mbarara. Grants will also be adjusted but it seems unlikely that Ankole will be much richer because it must pay to run its new responsibilities. The need to pay taxes is as great or greater than ever.

(g) The D.C. and his staff will continue much as at present except for the following changes:-

(1) Both the Government and the ordinary people will increasingly have to deal with the Ankole Native Government direct. The D.C. and his staff will still be available to listen to complaints but very often instead of dealing with the complaint ourselves we shall have to use our influence with the Native Government. People should always try and settle their complaints first with the Native Government.

(2) As already stated, the D.C. and his staff have nothing to do with courts.

(3) The D.C. and his staff retain the right to inspect all books and activities of the Native Government and report if they are failing to do their duty. Increasingly, however, we shall ask the Omubiiki's office to inspect the cash books.

The D.C. still retains overall responsibility for all those many services still run by Central Government, and in particular is directly responsible for law and order. This means that chiefs and the Native Government must obey an order given by the D.C. on this subject.

There are many other matters such as looking after refugees and running elections which will still be the responsibility of the D.C. because there is no other official available to do them.

D.C., Ankole

Annex 2: Handover Notes for Arms and Ammunition

ARMS AND AMMUNITION
Mr Wakhweya

1. *Procedure for dealing with applications for firearm certificates.*

The application forms should be kept by you and not in the General Office. You may not refuse to hand anyone the forms but this enables you to see who are going to make applications and to warn off those whose applications will clearly not be approved.

When the completed forms have been sent in you should:-

(a) Check that the form is properly completed and that the O.C. Police has signed at the foot of the form.

(b) Send the file to the Game Ranger and ask if he has any objections.

(c) Make enquiries concerning the position and reputation of the applicant. There is no need to write automatically to the referee as one assumes that they will support the application. In the case of Government Servants the opinion of the Applicant's Head of Department (locally) should be obtained. The Saza chief should be asked for an opinion when the applicant is an African unknown to you. Mr de Souza and Mr Gupta will usually be able to help in the case of Asians.

When writing the minute for the D.C. there is no need to express an opinion. The minute should contain a description of the applicant's position and reputation, in the case of Central Government and A.N.G. employees details of their service, the comments of the Game Ranger and the information whether or not the applicant has other firearms. (See minutes already in the files.)

If the application is approved, the forms should be collected from this office, not sent.

2. *Renewal of Firearm Certificates.*

The renewal forms should again be kept by you. Only one need be completed. The applicant should bring his firearm and the gun inspected to see that it is in sound mechanical condition. If there are obvious defects, the certificate should not be renewed. If you are in doubt about any gun, ask the Game Ranger for his opinion. Don't take risks as it may mean the loss of someone's life.

3. *Ammunition Permits.*

Local limits have been set down to the number of cartridges that may be issued on one certificate. These limits are known to the clerk who makes out the permits and if anyone should wish to exceed them, you should first obtain the agreement of the Game Ranger or in his absence, the D.C.

The only licensed firearm dealer in Mbarara is Sanitary, Hardware and Equipment Ltd. and one key of their store is kept by us. This store should be inspected with the O.C. Police at least twice a year. It was last inspected on 11 May 1962.

4. You should read the following:

(a) Administrative Instructions concerning firearms.
(b) The instructions regarding the licensing of visitors' firearms.
(c) The procedure for issuing Game Licences (this is often tied in with firearms).
(d) The descriptions of the Controlled Hunting Areas.

Annex 3: Letter of resignation

17th October, 1961.

The Permanent Secretary,
Office of the Chief Minister,
P.O. Box 5,
ENTEBBE.

      u.f.s. The Provincial Commissioner,
             Western Province, Fort Portal.

      u.f.s. The District Commissioner,
             Ankole District, Mbarara.

Sir,

      I shall have completed two years of my
present tour on 18th January, 1962, and should be
grateful if you would give your approval for my
tour to be extended to June, 1962.

2.   After considerable thought I have decided
not to continue working in Uganda after independence:
I am too junior to have any prospects of promotion
in Uganda but am still at an age when it should not
be difficult to begin another career. I should
therefore like to retire with compensation at the
end of my leave in November, 1962.

3.   I should prefer to extend my tour rather
than take leave after two years and return for a few
months, for two reasons. Firstly, as I have decided
not to stay after independence, I should like to
stay until after the elections in April, and secondly,
for personal reasons, in that most interviews take
place in the summer which would enable me to start
another career in 1962 rather than 1963.

               I am, Sir,
                Your obedient servant,

                  (P.J. Walker).
               District Officer.

Annex 4: 1985 Letter from Uganda Army Wives

UGANDA NATIONAL LIBERATION ARMY

24 Inf Battalion Tororo
P.O. Box 570
Tororo
July 1985

SPEECH OF WOMAN'S CLUB OF 24 BN TORORO
IN THE HONOUR OF HER BRITTANIC MAJESTIES,
ASSISTANT CHIEF OF DEFENCE STAFF AIR VICE
MARSAL JMD SUTTON.

1. We have great pleasure to receive you here in Tororo and in
our country Uganda at large. We really appreciate the work
being done by the British Government to enable her troops to
train our husbands.

2. We the women of 24 Bn Tororo are very much pleased with
Capt Limb and C/Sgt Hollinsherd who were sent here to train
our husbands. Since they arrived here in 24 Bn Tororo, they
have really shown the heart of brother wood and the training
they are giving our husbands shall never be forgotten. We
humbly beg the British Government through you to extend their
duration here in Tororo and also in Uganda for a long time.

3. Lastly, but not the least, we very much beg you to let Capt
Limb stay here in our Bn for at least 3 years so that our men
can gain the best discipline as that of the 1960s. Since Capt
Limb started training our men, we are very much happy because:-

    a. Our husbands don't disturb or beat us since they are
much engaged in Training.

    b. Our husbands do not go out to look for other lousy
women in Town as they are busy Training.

    c. They do not even drink as before since there is no
time for such luxuries.

4. CONCLUSION

From the above mentioned points forwarded to you, we the women
of 24 Bn Tororo, have given you a He-Goat. Take it, slaughter
it, when you are eating it, try to remember the extention of
duration for the BMATT in Uganda.

Thank you very much for calling on us, thank you in advance.

Mrs. Josephine Kilama
Chairman of Woman's Club of 24 Bn.

Index

A

Aga Khan, 120–21

Albers, Father Louis, Mill Hill
    Father 139–40

Alderney 6, 19, 54–7, 151, 192

Allen, Peter 129, 191

Athlone Castle 194–95

B

Barber James 72, 96

Barnes, Gerard 72, 118

Barnett, Lady 126

Barnwell, Hatch, Magistrate 82

Bataringaya, Basil 178, 183

Batten, Keith, District Medical
    Officer xi, 100, 113–14,
    135

Beith, Cecily 14, 53

Beith, Rob 14, 53, 67, 74

Bleach, Barrie 100, 141

Boyd, Limuru farmer 116–17,
    127

Buccaneers Cricket Club 58–9

Burglary in Mbarara 156,
    162–63

Burke, Fred and Daphne 114

Burnett, Ian 41, 43

Byamugisha, Jonathan 167,
    187, 203

C

Canopus Flying Boat 47

Champion, John 198

Clarence, Bill 72, 78, 112

Cohen, Sir Andrew, Governor
    93, 96–7

Colonial Office Resettlement
    Bureau 196–97

Congo refugees 171–73

Constitutional Committee
    145–47

Constitutional Conference 1961
    185

Cox, Tom, Provincial
    Commissioner 97, 139, 141

Cramb, Finlay, Headmaster
    Kenton College 35–6, 38

Crawford, Sir Frederick,
    Governor 115–16, 125,
    126

Cunningham, Edward xi, 90,
    94, 96, 126, 129

D

Davies, Mike 198

Democratic Party 177, 179, 183, 187, 199

Dening, Beadon 172

Dunnottar Castle 73–7

E

Egypt 52, 77

Eishengyero (District Council), Ankole 177–79

Ejoku, Enosi 125

Election of 1958 127–31

Election of 1961 182–83

Election of 1962 185–87

Eyudi, Salatieri (cook) 85–6, 147, 156, 188, 193

F

Fleming review of salaries 148

Fraser, Hugh, DC Ankole 142, 158, 165, 187, 196, 198

G

Gardner, Charles xi, 35

Good Hope Castle 56

Grief, Bishop of Tororo 20, 116

Griffith, Owen, DC Teso 77, 79, 84, 89, 100, 114, 117, 131, 149

Griffith, Rosemary 79, 88, 100, 126

H

Haddock, Fin, Veterinary Officer 102, 147

Hartwell, Sir Charles, Chief Secretary 124, 126

Hastings, Adrian, Priest Masaka Diocese 68, 156, 158

Hastings, Hazel, Mother-in-Law 61, 74, 99, 101, 133, 135, 200

Hastings, Peter 127

Herbert, Peter xi, 165

Hilders, Mill Hill Father 118

J

Jacobs, Jake, DC Lango 94, 95

Janurek, Jan and Peggy 65

Jones, Douglas, Tsetse Control Officer, Ankole, 187

K

Kaboha, John 72, 202, 203–4

Kalimuzo, Frank 72, 145, 175, 202

Kenton College, Nairobi xi, 35–44

Kings School, Canterbury 19, 36, 50–3

Kirkland Family, Nairobi 30–1

Kiwanuka, Benedict 174, 199

L

Lacey, dog 157–58

Lee, Basil 57

Leonard Cheshire xi, 98

LeFanu, Dick, British Council 190

Lira Riot 94–5

Ludya, ayah 87–9, 113, 135

M

Madera RC Mission 20, 139, 199

Malindi 45

Marshall, Don 84, 153

Matthew, Archbishop David 173

Matthews, David 74, 76, 77

Mbarara Club 158, 159

Mbarara plays 181, 188

McKinnon, Gordon 71, 72

Meister Omers, Kings School Canterbury 53

Munster Commission 183–85

N

Napak, Mount 143–145

Neilsen, Pop and Anna 136–39

Nganwa, NK, Enganzi, Ankole 178

No1, Ngong Road, Nairobi 26–9

Night Soil Porters, Soroti 91–2

Norris, Malcolm 76

Norris, Richard 61, 63–4

Nuti, Toni 190

Nzamisi Training Centre 93

O

Ogez, Jean-Marie, Bishop of Mbarara 179–80

Olding, Chris 72

Oxford University Air Squadron 65–6

P

Phelan, Maurice, Magistrate 156, 181

Plague epidemic 39–40

Prater, Raoul, piano teacher 36

Prior, RH (Sam) House Master 57, 59

Q

Queen Elizabeth National Park 159–61, 193

R

Rabone, John, Uncle 9

Resettlement, Ankole 164–76

Rhodesia Castle 193

Rwanda Refugees 173–76

S

Safari Routine 105–12

Salmon, Hugh 141

Sanderson, Ian 174, 189

Savage, John, Park Warden 112, 159–60

Sayers Road, Kuala Lumpur 17, 20

Scott, Ken 133, 143–45

Sempebwa, Earnest 73

Sheldon, Bernard 31

Shirley, Canon Frederick, Head Master 50, 57, 59

Singapore Mutiny, 1915 11–12

Sinclair Family, coffee farmers, 28, 127

Smith, Mure 76

Snoxall, Ron 73
Soroti Club 99–101, 135
South Africa 47–8
Straeter, Mill Hill Father 139
Strover, John 64
Sudan 51–2
T
Tamplin, Robin 178, 182
Tax Riot, Teso 131–32
Tew, Mary 173
Thompson, Rita,
    Governess 23–5, 30, 38,
    51, 119
Trinity College, Oxford 60–6
U
Uganda National Congress 94
Uganda People's Congress 179,
    183, 186, 187, 199
V
Vienna 57–8
W
Wakhweya, Emmanuel 158,
    187, 203
Walker, Adrian, Son 43, 72,
    83, 87–8, 99, 113–15,
    132 35, 189

Walker, Brian, Cousin 2
Walker, Cyril, Uncle xi, 2
Walker, Florence Ellen, Aunt 1
Walker, Gladys (née Rabone),
    Mother 5, 7–10, 16–19,
    192
Walker, Herbert, Uncle 2
Walker, Nicholas (Nick), Son
    100, 125, 127, 133–34,
    189, 194
Walker, Plumer Cosby,
    Grandfather 1, 2
Walker, Reginald Plumer,
    Father xi, 1, 5–7, 11–19,
    23, 30, 33, 48, 67, 120,
    192
Walker, William, Uncle 2
Watson, Arthur and Mary
    112, 129, 132, 145, 149
Westwood Park, Nairobi 37
Whitehorn, The Rev Roy 16,
    53, 57
Wild John 145, 202
Wright, Tony, Master, King's
    School Canterbury 57–8